THE SONG OF ROLAND

THE
SONG OF ROLAND

Translated by
C. K. SCOTT MONCRIEFF

With an Introduction by
G. K. CHESTERTON

And a Note on Technique by
GEORGE SAINTSBURY

ANN ARBOR PAPERBACKS
The University of Michigan Press

First edition as an Ann Arbor Paperback 1959
All rights reserved
Published in the United States of America by
the University of Michigan Press and simultaneously
in Toronto, Canada, by Ambassador Books, Ltd.

Manufactured in the United States of America

TO THREE MEN
SCHOLARS, POETS, SOLDIERS
WHO CAME TO THEIR RENCESVALS
IN SEPTEMBER, OCTOBER, AND NOVEMBER
NINETEEN HUNDRED AND EIGHTEEN
I DEDICATE MY PART IN A BOOK
OF WHICH THEIR FRIENDSHIP
QUICKENED THE BEGINNING
THEIR EXAMPLE HAS
JUSTIFIED THE CONTINUING

PHILIP BAINBRIGGE
WILFRED OWEN
IAN MACKENZIE

"Mare fustes, seignurs.
Tutes voz anmes ait Deus li glorius.
En Parèis les metet en seintes flurs."

Introduction

MOST of us remember reading, in the school histories of our childhood, that at the Battle of Hastings, Taillefer the Jongleur went in front of the Norman Army throwing his sword in the air and singing the Song of Roland. They were naturally histories of a very Victorian sort, which passed lightly over the Roman Empire and the Crusades on the way to serious things, such as the genealogy of George i or the administration of Addington. But that one image emerged in the imagination as something alive in its dead surroundings; like finding a familiar face in a faded tapestry. The song he sang, it is needless to say, was presumably not the noble and rugged epic which Captain Scott Moncrieff has done so solid and even historic a service to letters in rendering in its entirety. The jongleur must at least have selected extracts or favourite passages, or the battle would have been unduly delayed. But the tale has the same moral as the translation; since both have the same inspiration. The value of the tale was that it did suggest to the childish mind, through all the deadening effects of distance and indifference, that a man does not make such a gesture with a sword unless he feels something, and that a man does not sing unless he has something to sing about. Dull avarice and an appetite for feudal lands do not inspire such jugglery. In short, the value of the tale was that it hinted that there is a heart in history, even remote history. And the value of the translation is that if we are really to learn history we must, in a double sense of the word, learn it by heart. We must learn it at length and as it were at large; lingering over chance spaces of contemporary work, for love of its detail and one might almost say for love of its dulness. Even a random reader like myself, only dipping here and there into such things, so long as they are really things of the period, can often learn more from them than from the most careful constitutional digests or political summaries, by modern men more learned than himself. I admire the abnegation of the translator, who is himself a very brilliant and individual writer, in having really translated the Song of Roland. It would have been easy for a man of his poetic gift to make out of it a modern poem. It might easily have been a temptation to him to deal with Roland rather as Tennyson dealt with Arthur. But the value of his vivid and very laborious service to literature is precisely that a modern man, educated on the modern histories, may find here the things he does not expect. I have here only space for one example, out of many that I could give to show what I mean. Most of the stock histories tell the young student something of what Feudalism was in legal form and custom ; that the subordinates were called vassals, that they did homage and so on. But they do it somehow in such a way as to suggest a savage and sullen obedience ; as if a vassal were no more than a serf. What is left out is the fact that the homage really was homage ; a thing worthy of a man. The first feudal feeling had something ideal and even impersonal like patriotism. The nations were not yet born ; and these smaller groups had almost the souls of nations. Now in this translation, merely because it is an honest translation, the reader will find the word " vassalage " used again and again, on a note which is not only heroic but even haughty. The vassal is obviously as proud of being a vassal as anybody could be of being a lord. Indeed the feudal poet uses the word " vassalage " where a modern poet would use the word " chivalry." The Paladins charging the Paynims are spurred on by vassalage. Turpin the Archbishop hacks the Moslem chieftain rib from rib ; and the Christians, beholding his triumph, cry aloud in their pride that he has shown great vassalage ; and that with such an Archbishop the Cross is safe. There were no Conscientious Objections in their Christianity.

This a type of the truths that historical literature ought to make us feel ; but which mere histories very seldom do. The one example I have already given, of the Jongleur at Hastings, is a complexity of curious truths that might be conveyed and which very seldom are. We might have learned, for instance, what a Jongleur was ; and realised that this one may have had feelings as deep or fantastic as the Jongleur celebrated in the twelfth century poem, who died gloriously of dancing and turning somersaults before the image of Our Lady ; that he was of the trade taken as a type by the mystical mirth of St. Francis, who called his monks the Jugglers of God. A man must read at least a little of the contemporary work itself, before he thus finds the human heart inside the armour and the monastic gown ; the men who write the philosophy of history seldom give us the philosophy, still less the religion, of the historical characters. And the final example of this is something which is also illustrated by the obscure minstrel who threw up his sword as he sang the Song of Roland, as well as by the Song of Roland itself. Modern history, mainly ethnological or economic, always talks of a thing like the Norman adventure in the somewhat vulgar language of success. For these it is well to note, in the real Norman story, that the very bard in front of their battle line was shouting the glorification of failure. It testifies to a truth in the very heart of Christendom, that even the court poet of William the Conqueror was celebrating Roland the conquered.

That high note of the forlorn hope, of a host at bay and a battle against odds without end, is the note on which the great French epic ends. I know nothing more moving in poetry than that strange and unexpected ending ; that splendidly inconclusive conclusion. Charlemagne the Christian emperor has at last established his empire in quiet; has done justice almost in the manner of a day of judgement, and sleeps as it were upon his throne with a peace almost like that of Paradise. And there appears to him the angel of God crying aloud that his arms are needed in a new and distant land, and that he must take up again the endless march of his days. And the great king tears his long white beard and cries out against his restless life. The poem ends, as it were with a vision and vista of wars against the barbarians ; and the vision is true. For that war is never ended, which defends the sanity of the world against all the stark anarchies and rending negations which rage against it for ever. That war is never finished in this world ; and the grass has hardly grown on the graves of our own friends who fell in it.

G. K. CHESTERTON.

The Song of Roland

I

Charles the King, our Emperour the great,
Full seven years hath sojournèd in Spain,
Unto the sea conquered the lofty plain ;
Now no fortress against him doth remain,
No city walls are left for him to break,
Save Sarraguce, that sits on high mountain.
Marsile its king, who feareth not God's name,
Mahumet's man, he invokes Apollin's aid,
Nor wards off ills that shall to him attain.

II

King Marsilies he lay at Sarraguce,
Went he his way into an orchard cool ;
On a terrace he sate, of marble blue,
Round him his men, full twenty thousand, stood.
Called he forth then his counts, also his dukes :
" My Lords, give ear to our impending doom :
That Emperour, Charlès of France the Douce,
Into this land is come, us to confuse.
I have no host in battle him to prove,
Nor have I strength his forces to undo.
Counsel me then, ye that are wise and true ;
Can ye ward off this present death and dule ? "
What word to say no pagan of them knew,
Save Blancandrins, of th' Castle of Val Funde.

III

Blancandrins was a pagan very wise,
In vassalage he was a gallant knight,
First in prowess, he stood his lord beside.
And thus he spoke : " Do not yourself affright !
Yield to Carlun, that is so big with pride,
Faithful service, his friend and his ally ;
Lions and bears and hounds for him provide,
Thousand mewed hawks, sev'n hundred camelry;
Silver and gold, four hundred mules load high ;

Fifty wagons his wrights will need supply,
Till with that wealth he pays his soldiery.
35 War hath he waged in Spain too long a time,
To Aix, in France, homeward he will him hie.
Follow him there before Saint Michael's tide,
You shall receive and hold the Christian rite ;
Stand honour bound, and do him fealty.
40 Send hostages, should he demand surety,
Ten or a score, our loyal oath to bind ;
Send him our sons, the first-born of our wives;—
An he be slain, I'll surely furnish mine.
Better by far they go, though doomed to die,
45 Than that we lose honour and dignity,
And be ourselves brought down to beggary."

IV

Says Blancandrins : " By my right hand, I say,
And by this beard, that in the wind doth sway,
The Frankish host you'll see them all away ;
50 Franks will retire to France their own terrain.
When they are gone, to each his fair domain,
In his Chapelle at Aix will Charlès stay,
High festival will hold for Saint Michael.
Time will go by, and pass the appointed day ;
55 Tidings of us no Frank will hear or say.
Proud is that King, and cruel his courage ;
From th' hostages he'll slice their heads away.
Better by far their heads be shorn away,
Than that ourselves lose this clear land of Spain,
60 Than that ourselves do suffer grief and pain."
" That is well said. So be it." the pagans say.

V

The council ends, and that king Marsilie
Calleth aside Clarun of Balaguee,
Estramarin and Eudropin his peer,
65 And Priamun and Guarlan of the beard,
And Machiner and his uncle Mahee,
With Joüner, Malbien from over sea,

And Blancandrin, good reason to decree:
Ten hath he called, were first in felony.
70 " Gentle Barons, to Charlemagne go ye;
He is in siege of Cordres the city.
In your right hands bear olive-branches green
Which signify Peace and Humility.
If you by craft contrive to set me free,
75 Silver and gold, you'll have your fill of me,
Manors and fiefs, I'll give you all your need."
" We have enough," the pagans straight agree.

VI

King Marsilies, his council finishing,
Says to his men : " Go now, my lords, to him,
80 Olive-branches in your right hands bearing;
Bid ye for me that Charlemagne, the King,
In his God's name to shew me his mercy;
Ere this new moon wanes, I shall be with him;
One thousand men shall be my following;
85 I will receive the rite of christening,
Will be his man, my love and faith swearing;
Hostages too, he'll have, if so he will."
Says Blancandrins : " Much good will come
        of this."

VII

Ten snow-white mules then ordered Marsilie,
90 Gifts of a king, the king of Suatilie.
Bridled with gold, saddled in silver clear;
Mounted them those that should the message
        speak,
In their right hands were olive-branches green.
Came they to Charle, that holds all France in
        fee,
95 Yet cannot guard himself from treachery.

VIII

Merry and bold is now that Emperour,
Cordres he holds, the walls are tumbled down,

3

His catapults have battered town and tow'r.
Great good treasure his knights have placed in
    pound,
100   Silver and gold and many a jewelled gown.
In that city there is no pagan now
But he been slain, or takes the Christian vow.
The Emperour is in a great orchard ground
Where Oliver and Rollant stand around,
105   Sansun the Duke and Anséis the proud,
Gefreid d'Anjou, that bears his gonfaloun ;
There too Gerin and there Geriers are found.
Where they are found, is seen a mighty crowd,
Fifteen thousand, from France the Douce come
    out.
110   On white carpets those knights have sate them
    down,
At the game-boards to pass an idle hour ;—
Chequers the old, for wisdom most renowned
While fence the young and lusty bachelours.
Beneath a pine, in eglantine embow'red,
115   Stands a fald-stool, fashioned of gold throughout;
There sits the King, that holds Douce France in
    pow'r ;
White is his beard, and blossoming-white his
    crown,
Shapely his limbs, his countenance is proud.
Should any seek, no need to point him out.
120   The messengers, on foot they get them down,
And in salute full courteously they lout.

IX

The foremost word of all Blancandrin spake,
And to the King : " May God preserve you safe,
The All Glorious, to Whom ye're bound to pray!
125   Proud Marsilies this message bids me say :
Much hath he sought to find salvation's way ;
Out of his wealth meet presents would he make,
Lions and bears, and greyhounds leashed on
    chain,

4

Thousand mewed hawks, sev'n hundred drome-
            drays,
130 Four hundred mules his silver shall convey,
Fifty wagons you'll need to bear away
Golden besants, such store of proved assay,
Wherewith full tale your soldiers you can pay.
Now in this land you've been too long a day ;
135 Hie you to France, return again to Aix ;
Thus saith my lord, he'll follow too that way."
That Emperour t'wards God his arms he raised
Lowered his head, began to meditate.

X

That Emperour inclined his head full low ;
140 Hasty in speech he never was, but slow :
His custom was, at his leisure he spoke.
When he looks up, his face is very bold,
He says to them : " Good tidings have you told.
King Marsilies hath ever been my foe.
145 These very words you have before me told,
In what measure of faith am I to hold ? "
That Sarrazin says, " Hostages he'll show ;
Ten shall you take, or fifteen or a score.
Though he be slain, a son of mine shall go,
150 Any there be you'll have more nobly born.
To your palace seigneurial when you go,
At Michael's Feast, called *in periculo ;*
My Lord hath said, thither will he follow
Ev'n to your baths, that God for you hath
            wrought ;
155 There is he fain the Christian faith to know."
Answers him Charles : " Still may he heal his
            soul."

XI

Clear shone the sun in a fair even-tide ;
Those ten men's mules in stall he bade them tie.
Also a tent in the orchard raise on high,
160 Those messengers had lodging for the night ;
Dozen serjeants served after them aright.
Darkling they lie till comes the clear daylight.

5

That Emperour does with the morning rise ;
Matins and Mass are said then in his sight.
165 Forth goes that King, and stays beneath a pine ;
Barons he calls, good counsel to define,
For with his Franks he's ever of a mind.

XII

That Emperour, beneath a pine he sits,
Calls his barons, his council to begin :
170 Oger the Duke, that Archbishop Turpin,
Richard the old, and his nephew Henry,
From Gascony the proof Count Acelin,
Tedbald of Reims and Milun his cousin :
With him there were Gerers, also Gerin,
175 And among them the Count Rollanz came in,
And Oliver, so proof and so gentil.
Franks out of France, a thousand chivalry ;
Guenès came there, that wrought the treachery.
The Council then began, which ended ill.

XIII

180 " My Lords Barons," says the Emperour then,
Charlès,
" King Marsilies hath sent me his messages ;
Out of his wealth he'll give me weighty masses.
Greyhounds on leash and bears and lions also,
Thousand mewed hawks and seven hundred
camels,
185 Four hundred mules with gold Arabian chargèd,
Fifty wagons, yea more than fifty drawing.
But into France demands he my departure ;
He'll follow me to Aix, where is my Castle ;
There he'll receive the law of our Salvation :
190 Christian he'll be, and hold from me his marches.
But I know not what purpose in his heart is."
Then say the Franks : " Beseems us act with
caution ! "

6

XIV

That Emperour hath ended now his speech.
The Count Rollanz, he never will agree,
195 Quick to reply, he springs upon his feet ;
And to the King, " Believe not Marsilie.
Seven years since, when into Spain came we,
I conquer'd you Noples also Commibles,
And took Valterne, and all the land of Pine,
200 And Balaguet, and Tuele, and Sezilie.
Traitor in all his ways was Marsilies ;
Of his pagans he sent you then fifteen,
Bearing in hand their olive-branches green ;
Who, ev'n as now, these very words did speak.
205 You of your Franks a Council did decree,
Praised they your words that foolish were in deed.
Two of your Counts did to the pagan speed,
Basan was one, and the other Basilie :
Their heads he took on th' hill by Haltilie.
210 War have you waged, so on to war proceed,
To Sarraguce lead forth your great army.
All your life long, if need be, lie in siege,
Vengeance for those the felon slew to wreak."

XV

That Emperour he sits with low'ring front,
215 He clasps his chin, his beard his fingers tug,
Good word nor bad, his nephew hears not one.
Franks hold their peace, but only Guenelun
Springs to his feet, and comes before Carlun ;
Right haughtily his reason he's begun,
220 And to the King : " Believe not any one,
My word nor theirs, save whence your good shall
come.
Since he sends word, that king Marsiliun,
Homage he'll do, by finger and by thumb ;
Throughout all Spain your writ alone shall run ;
225 Next he'll receive our rule of Christendom ;
Who shall advise, this bidding be not done,

7

Deserves not death, since all to death must come.
Counsel of pride is wrong : we've fought enough.
Leave we the fools, and with the wise be one."

XVI

230 And after him came Neimès out, the third,
Better vassal there was not in the world ;
And to the King : " Now rightly have you heard
Guenès the Count, what answer he returned.
Wisdom was there, but let it well be heard.
235 King Marsilies in war is overturned,
His castles all in ruin have you hurled,
With catapults his ramparts have you burst,
Vanquished his men, and all his cities burned ;
Him who entreats your pity do not spurn,
240 Sinners were they that would to war return ;
With hostages his faith he would secure ;
Let this great war no longer now endure."
" Well said the Duke." Franks utter in their turn.

XVII

" My lords barons, say whom shall we send up
245 To Sarraguce, to king Marsiliun ? "
Answers Duke Neimes : " I'll go there for your
love ;
Give me therefore the wand, also the glove."
Answers the King : " Old man of wisdom pruff ;
By this white beard, and as these cheeks are rough,
250 You'll not this year so far from me remove ;
Go sit you down, for none hath called you up."

XVIII

" My lords barons, say whom now can we send
To th' Sarrazin that Sarraguce defends ? "
Answers Rollanz : " I might go very well."
255 " Certes, you'll not," says count Olivier then,
" For your courage is cruel in its strength ;
I am afraid you would not long be friends.
If the King wills it I might go there well."
Answers the King : " Be silent both on bench ;

260   Your feet nor his, I say, shall that way wend.
Nay, by this beard, that you have seen grow
     blench,
'The dozen peers it would be wrong to send.
Franks hold their peace ; you'd seen them all
     silent.

XIX

Turpins of Reins is risen from his rank,
265   Says to the King : " In peace now leave your
     Franks.
For seven years you've lingered in this land ;
They have endured much pain and sufferance.
Give, Sire, to me the glove, also the wand,
I will seek out the Spanish Sarazand,
270   What's in my mind I'll make him understand."
That Emperour answers intolerant :
" Go, sit you down on yonder silken mat ;
And speak no more, until that I command."

XX

" Franks, chevaliers," says the Emperour then,
     Charlès,
275   " Choose ye me out a baron from my marches,
To Marsilie shall carry back my answer."
Then says Rollanz : " 'There's Guenès, my good-
     father.''*
Answer the Franks : " For he can wisely man-
     age ;
So let him go, there's none you should send
     rather."
280   And that count Guenes is very full of anguish ;
Off from his neck he flings the pelts of marten,
And on his feet stands clear in silken garment.
Proud face he had, his eyes with colour sparkled ;
Fine limbs he had, his ribs were broadly archèd ;

---

* M. Gautier has re-arranged this passage as follows :
lines 276, additional line, 277, 279, 278, additional line ;
laisse xxiv, xxiii, lines 280-295, laisses xxi, xxii, additional
laisse, xxv, etc.

285 So fair he seemed that all the court regarded.
Says to Rollant : " Fool, wherefore art so wrath-
ful ?
All men know well that I am thy good-father ;
Thou hast decreed, to Marsiliun I travel.
Then if God grant that I return hereafter,
290 I'll follow thee with such a force of passion
That will endure so long as life may last thee."
Answers Rollanz : " Thou'rt full of pride and
madness.
All men know well, I take no thought for slander;
But some wise man, surely, should bear the
answer ;
295 If the King will, I'm ready to go rather."

XXI

Answers him Guene : " Thou shalt not go for
me.
Thou'rt not my man, nor am I lord of thee.
Charlès commands that I do his decree,
To Sarraguce going to Marsilie ;
300 There I will work a little trickery,
This mighty wrath of mine I'll thus let free."
When Rollanz heard, began to laugh for glee.

XXII

When Guenès sees that Rollant laughs at it,
Such grief he has, for rage he's like to split,
305 A little more, and he has lost his wit :
Says to that count : " I love you not a bit ;
A false judgement you bore me when you chid.
Right Emperour, you see me where you sit,
I will your word accomplish, as you bid.

XXIII

310 " To Sarraguce I must repair, 'tis plain ;
Whence who goes there returns no more again.

10

Your sister's hand in marriage have I ta'en ;
And I've a son, there is no prettier swain :
Baldwin, men say he shews the knightly strain
315 To him I leave my honours and domain.
Care well for him ; he'll look for me in vain."
Answers him Charles : " Your heart is too
humane.
When I command, time is to start amain."

XXIV

Then says the King : " Guenès, before me
stand ;
320 And take from me the glove, also the wand.
For you have heard, you're chosen by the Franks,
" Sire," answers Guenes, " all this is from
Rollanz ;
I'll not love him, so long as I'm a man,
Nor Oliver, who goes at his right hand ;
325 The dozen peers, for they are of his band,
All I defy, as in your sight I stand."
Then says the King : " Over intolerant.
Now certainly you go when I command."
" And go I can ; yet have I no warrant ;
330 Basile had none, nor his brother Basant."

XXV

His right hand glove that Emperour holds out ,
But the count Guenes elsewhere would fain be
found ;
When he should take, it falls upon the ground.
Murmur the Franks : " God ! What may that
mean now ?
335 By this message great loss shall come about."
" Lordings," says Guene, " You'll soon have
news enow."

XXVI

" Now," Guenès said, " give me your orders,
Sire ;

11

Since I must go, why need I linger, I ? "
Then said the King : " In Jesu's Name and
   mine ! "
340. With his right hand he has absolved and signed,
Then to his care the wand and brief confides.

XXVII

Guenès the count goes to his hostelry,
Finds for the road his garments and his gear,
All of the best he takes that may appear :
345 Spurs of fine gold he fastens on his feet,
And to his side Murglès his sword of steel.
On Tachebrun, his charger, next he leaps,
His uncle holds the stirrup, Guinemere.
Then you had seen so many knights to weep,
350 Who all exclaim : " Unlucky lord, indeed !
In the King's court these many years you've
   been,
Noble vassal, they say that have you seen.
He that for you this journey has decreed
King Charlemagne will never hold him dear.
355 The Count Rollant, he should not so have deemed,
Knowing you were born of very noble breed."
After they say : " Sire, let us too proceed ! "
Then answers Guenes : " Not so, the Lord be
   pleased !
Far better one than many knights should bleed.
360 To France the Douce, my lords, you soon shall
   speed,
On my behalf my gentle wife you'll greet,
And Pinabel, who is my friend and peer,
And Baldëwin, my son, whom you have seen ;
His rights accord and help him in his need."
365 —Rides down the road, and on his way goes he.

XXVIII

Guenes canters on, and halts beneath a tree ;
Where Sarrazins assembled he may see,
With Blancandrins, who abides his company.

12

Cunning and keen they speak then, each to each,
370 Says Blancandrins : " Charles, what a man is he,
Who conquered Puille and th'whole of Calabrie ;
Into England he crossed the bitter sea,
To th' holy Pope restored again his fee.
What seeks he now of us in our country ? "
375 Then answers Guene : " So great courage hath
         he ;
Never was man against him might succeed."

XXIX

Says Blancandrins : " Gentle the Franks are
         found ;
Yet a great wrong these dukes do and these
         counts
Unto their lord, being in counsel proud ;
380 Him and themselves they harry and confound."
Answers him Guene : " There is none such,
         without
Only Rollanz, whom shame will yet find out.
Once in the shade the King had sate him down ;
His nephew came, in sark of iron brown,
385 Spoils he had won, beyond by Carcasoune,
Held in his hand an apple red and round.
" Behold, fair Sire," said Rollanz as he bowed,
" Of all earth's kings I bring you here the crowns."
" His cruel pride must shortly him confound,
390 Each day t'wards death he goes a little down,
When he be slain, shall peace once more abound."

XXX

Says Blancandrins : " A cruel man, Rollant,
That would bring down to bondage every man,
And challenges the peace of every land.
395 With what people takes he this task in hand ? "
And answers Guene : " The people of the
         Franks ;
They love him so, for men he'll never want.
Silver and gold he show'rs upon his band,

13

Chargers and mules, garments and silken mats.
400 The King himself holds all by his command ;
From hence to the East he'll conquer sea and
    land."

XXXI

Cantered so far then Blancandrins and Guene
Till each by each a covenant had made
And sought a plan, how Rollant might be slain.
405 Cantered so far by valley and by plain
To Sarraguce beneath a cliff they came.
There a fald-stool stood in a pine-tree's shade,
Enveloped all in Alexandrin veils ;
There was the king that held the whole of
    Spain,
410 Twenty thousand of Sarrazins his train ;
Nor was there one but did his speech contain,
Eager for news, till they might hear the tale.
Haste into sight then Blancandrins and Guene.

XXXII

Blancandrin comes before Marsiliun,
415 Holding the hand of county Guenelun ;
Says to the king : " Lord save you, Sire, Mahum
And Apollin, whose holy laws here run ! "
Your message we delivered to Charlun,
Both his two hands he raised against the sun,
420 Praising his God, but answer made he none.
He sends you here his noblest born barun,
Greatest in wealth, that out of France is come ;
From him you'll hear if peace shall be, or none."
" Speak," said Marsile : " We'll hear him, every
    one."

XXXIII

425 But the count Guenes did deeply meditate ;
Cunning and keen began at length, and spake
Even as one that knoweth well the way ;
And to the king : " May God preserve you safe,
The All Glorious, to whom we're bound to pray.

14

430 Proud Charlemagne this message bids me say :
You must receive the holy Christian Faith :
He'll give you in fee one half the land of Spain.
If to accord this tribute you disdain,
Taken by force and bound by might and main ;
435 You will be brought before his throne at Aix ;
Judged and condemned you'll be, and shortly
    slain,
Yes, you will die in misery and shame."
King ¦Marsilies was very sore afraid,
Snatching a dart, with golden feathers gay,
440 He made to strike : they turned aside his aim.

XXXIV

King Marsilies is turnèd white with rage,
His feathered dart he brandishes and shakes.
Guenès beholds : his sword in hand he takes,
Two fingers' width from scabbard bares the
    blade ;
445 And says to it : " O clear and fair and brave ;
Before this king in court we'll so behave,
That the Emperour of France shall never say
In a strange land I'd thrown my life away
Before these chiefs thy temper had essayed."
450 " Let us prevent this fight : " the pagans say.

XXXV

The best of them did so much him beseech,
On the fald-stool Marsillies took his seat.
" Greatly you harm our cause," says the alcaliph :
" When on this Frank your vengeance you would
    wreak ;
455 Rather you should listen to hear him speak."
" Sire," Guenès says, " to suffer I am meek.
I will not fail, for all the gold God keeps,
Nay, should this land its treasure pile in heaps,
But I will tell, so long as I be free,
460 What Charlemagne, that Royal Majesty,
Bids me inform his mortal enemy."

*   *   *   *

15

Guenès had on a cloke of sable skin,
And over it a veil Alexandrin ;
These he throws down, they're held by Blan-
    candrin ;
465   But not his sword. he'll not leave hold of it,
In his right hand he grasps the golden hilt.
The pagans say . " A noble baron, this."

XXXVI

Before the king's face Guenès drawing near
Says to him : " Sire, wherefore this rage and
    fear ?
470   Seeing you are, by Charles, of Franks the chief,
Bidden to hold the Christians' right belief.
One half of Spain he'll render as your fief,
The rest Rollanz, his nephew, shall receive,
Proud parcener in him you'll have indeed.
475   If you will not to Charles this tribute cede,
To you he'll come, and Sarraguce besiege ;
Take you by force, and bind you hands and feet,
Bear you outright ev'n unto Aix his seat.
You will not then on palfrey nor on steed,
480   Jennet nor mule, come cantering in your speed ;
Flung you will be on a vile sumpter-beast ;
Tried there and judged, your head you will not
    keep.
Our Emperour has sent you here this brief."
He's given it into the pagan's nief.

XXXVII

485   Now Marsilies is turnèd white with ire,
He breaks the seal and casts the wax aside,
Looks in the brief, sees what the King did write :
" Charlès commands, who holds all France by
    might,
I bear in mind his bitter grief and ire ;
490   'Tis of Basan and 's brother Basilye,
Whose heads I took on th' hill by Haltilye.

16

If I would save my body now alive,
I must despatch my uncle the alcalyph,
Charles will not love me ever otherwise."
495 After, there speaks his son to Marsilye,
Says to the king : " In madness spoke this
wight.
So wrong he was, to spare him were not right ;
Leave him to me, I will that wrong requite."
When Guenès hears, he draws his sword out-
right,
500 Against the trunk he stands, beneath that pine.

XXXVIII

The king is gone into that orchard then ;
With him he takes the best among his men ;
And Blancandrins there shews his snowy hair,
And Jursalet, was the king's son and heir,
505 And the alcaliph, his uncle and his friend.
Says Blancandrins : " Summon the Frank again,
In our service his faith to me he's pledged."
Then says the king : " So let him now be
fetched."
He's taken Guenes by his right finger-ends,
510 And through the orchard straight to the King
they wend.
Of treason there make lawless parliament.

XXXIX

" Fair Master Guenes," says then king Marsilie,
" I did you now a little trickery,
Making to strike, I shewed my great fury.
515 These sable skins I'll have you take from me ;
Five hundred pounds would not their worth
redeem.
To-morrow night a fair amends they'll seem."
Guene answers him : " I'll not refuse it, me.
May God be pleased to shew you His mercy."

17

520 Then says Marsile : " Guenès, the truth to ken,
Minded I am to love you very well.
Of Charlemagne I wish to hear you tell,
He's very old, his time is nearly spent,
Two hundred years he's lived now, as 'tis said.
525 Through many lands his armies he has led,
So many blows his buckled shield has shed,
And so rich kings he's brought to beg their
bread ;
What time from war will he draw back instead ?"
And answers Guenes : " Not so was Charlès bred.
530 There is no man that sees and knows him well
But will proclaim the Emperour's hardihead.
Praise him as best I may, when all is said,
Remain untold, honour and goodness yet.
His great valour how can it be counted ?
535 Him with such grace hath God illuminèd,
Better to die than leave his banneret.

The pagan says : " You make me marvel sore
At Charlemagne, who is so old and hoar ;
Two hundred years, they say, he's lived and more.
540 So many lands he's led his armies o'er,
So many blows from spears and lances borne,
And so rich kings brought down to beg and sorn,
When will time come that he draws back from
war ? "

*   *   *   *

" Never," says Guenes, " so long as lives his
nephew ;
545 No such vassal goes neath the dome of heaven ;
And proof also is Oliver his henchman ;
The dozen peers, whom Charlès holds so precious,
These are his guards, with other thousands
twenty.
Charles is secure, he holds no man in terror."

XLII

550 Says Sarrazin : " My wonder yet is grand
At Charlemagne, who hoary is and blanched.
Two hundred years and more, I understand,
He has gone forth and conquered many a land,
Such blows hath borne from many a trenchant
lance,
555 Vanquished and slain of kings so rich a band,
When will time come that he from war draws
back ? "
" Never," says Guene, " so long as lives Rollanz,
From hence to the East there is no such vassal ;
And proof also, Oliver his comrade ;
560 The dozen peers he cherishes at hand,
These are his guard, with twenty thousand
Franks.
Charles is secure, he fears no living man."

XLIII

" Fair Master Guenes," says Marsilies the king,
Such men are mine, fairer than tongue can sing,
565 Of knights I can four hundred thousand bring
So I may fight with Franks and with their King."
Answers him Guenes : " Not on this journey-
ing !
Save of pagans a great loss suffering.
Leave you the fools, wise counsel following ;
570 To the Emperour such wealth of treasure give
That every Frank at once is marvelling.
For twenty men that you shall now send in
To France the Douce he will repair, that King ;
In the rereward will follow after him
575 Both his nephew, count Rollant, as I think,
And Oliver, that courteous paladin ;
Dead are the counts, believe me if you will.
Charles will behold his great pride perishing,
For battle then he'll have no more the skill."

XLIV

580　　" Fair Master Guene," says then king Marsilie,
　　　　Shew the device, how Rollant slain may be."
　　　　Answers him Guenes : " That will I soon make
　　　　　　clear :
　　　　The King will cross by the good pass of Size,
　　　　A guard he'll set behind him, in the rear ;
585　　His nephew there, count Rollant, that rich peer,
　　　　And Oliver, in whom he well believes ;
　　　　Twenty thousand Franks in their company.
　　　　Five score thousand pagans upon them lead,
　　　　Franks unawares in battle you shall meet,
590　　Bruisèd and bled the race of Franks shall be ;
　　　　I do not say, but yours shall also bleed.
　　　　Battle again deliver, and with speed.
　　　　So, first or last, from Rollant you'll be freed.
　　　　You will have wrought a high chivalrous deed,
595　　Nor all your life know war again, but peace."

XLV

　　　　" Could one achieve that Rollant's life was lost,
　　　　Charlè's right arm were from his body torn ;
　　　　Though there remained his marvellous great
　　　　　　host,
　　　　He'ld not again assemble in such force ;
600　　Terra Major would languish in repose."
　　　　Marsile has heard, he's kissed him on the throat ;
　　　　Next he begins to undo his treasure-store.

XLVI

　　　　Said Marsilie—but now what more said they ?—
　　　　" No faith in words by oath unbound I lay ;
605　　Swear me the death of Rollant on that day."
　　　　Then answered Guene : " So be it, as you say."
　　　　On the relics, are in his sword Murglès,
　　　　Treason he's sworn, forsworn his faith away.

20

XLVII

Was a fald-stool there, made of olifant.
610 A book thereon Marsilies bade them plant,
In it their laws, Mahum's and Tervagant's.
He's sworn thereby, the Spanish Sarazand,
In the rereward if he shall find Rollant,
Battle to give, himself and all his band,
615 And verily he'll slay him if he can.
And answered Guenes : " So be it, as you com-
      mand ! "

XLVIII

In haste there came a pagan, Valdabrun,
Warden had been to king Marsiliun,
Smiling and clear, he's said to Guenelun,
620 " Take now this sword, and better sword has
      none ;
Into the hilt a thousand coins are run.
To you, fair sir, I offer it in love ;
Give us your aid from Rollant the barun,
That in rereward against him we may come."
625 Guenès the count answers : " It shall be done."
Then, cheek and chin, kissed each the other one.

XLIX

After there came a pagan, Climorins,
Smiling and clear to Guenelun begins :
" Take now my helm, better is none than this ;
630 But give us aid, on Rollant the marquis,
By what device we may dishonour bring."
" It shall be done." Count Guenès answered
      him ;
On mouth and cheek then each the other kissed.

L

In haste there came the queen forth, Brami-
      mound ;
635 " I love you well, sir," said she to the count,
" For prize you dear my lord and all around ;

Here for you wife I have two brooches found,
Amethysts and jacynths in golden mounts ;
More worth are they than all the wealth of Roum;
640 Your Emperour has none such, I'll be bound."
He's taken them, and in his hosen pouched.

LI

The king now calls Malduiz, that guards his
    treasure.
" Tribute for Charles, say, is it now made ready?"
He answers him : " Ay, Sire, for here is plenty :
645 Silver and gold on hundred camels seven,
And twenty men, the gentlest under heaven."

LII

Marsilie's arm Guene's shoulder doth enfold ;
He's said to him : " You are both wise and bold.
Now, by the law that you most sacred hold,
650 Let not your heart in our behalf grow cold !
Out of my store I'll give you wealth untold,
Charging ten mules with fine Arabian gold ;
I'll do the same for you, new year and old.

*   *   *   *

Take then the keys of this city so large,
655 This great tribute present you first to Charles,
Then get me placed Rollanz in the rereward.
If him I find in valley or in pass,
Battle I'll give him that shall be the last."
Answers him Guenes : " My time is nearly
    past."
660 His charger mounts, and on his journey starts.

LIII

That Emperour draws near to his domain,
He is come down unto the city Gailne.
The Count Rollanz had broken it and ta'en,
An hundred years its ruins shall remain.

22

665 Of Guenelun the King for news is fain,
And for tribute from the great land of Spain.
At dawn of day, just as the light grows plain,
Into their camp is come the county Guene.

LIV

In morning time is risen the Emperere,
670 Mattins and Mass he's heard, and made his prayer;
On the green grass before the tent his chair,
Where Rollant stood and that bold Oliver,
Neimès the Duke, and many others there.
Guenès arrived, the felon perjurer,
675 Begins to speak, with very cunning air,
Says to the King : " God keep you, Sire, I
swear !
Of Sarraguce the keys to you I bear,
Tribute I bring you, very great and rare,
And twenty men ; look after them with care.
680 Proud Marsilies bade me this word declare :
That the alcaliph, his uncle, you must spare.
My own eyes saw four hundred thousand there,
In hauberks dressed, closed helms that gleamed
in the air,
And golden hilts upon their swords they bare.
685 They followed him, right to the sea they'ld fare ;
Marsile they left, that would their faith forswear,
For Christendom they've neither wish nor care.
But the fourth league they had not compassed,
ere
Brake from the North tempest and storm in the
air ;
690 Then were they drowned, they will no more
appear.
Were he alive, I should have brought him here.
The pagan king, in truth, Sire, bids you hear,
Ere you have seen one month pass of this year
He'll follow you to France, to your Empire,
695 He will accept the laws you hold and fear ;
Joining his hands, will do you homage there,

23

Kingdom of Spain will hold as you declare."
Then says the King : " Now God be praised, I
  swear !
Well have you wrought, and rich reward shall
  wear."
700 Bids through the host a thousand trumpets blare.
Franks leave their lines ; the sumpter-beasts
  are yare ;
T'wards France the Douce all on their way
  repair.

LV

Charlès the Great that land of Spain had wasted,
Her castles ta'en, her cities violated.
705 Then said the King, his war was now abated.
Towards Douce France that Emperour has hasted.
Upon a lance Rollant his ensign raisèd,
High on a cliff against the sky 'twas placèd ;
The Franks in camp through all that country
  baited.
710 Cantered pagans, through those wide valleys
  racèd,
Hauberks they wore, their sarks were doubly
  plated,
Swords to their sides were girt, their helms were
  lacèd,
Lances made sharp, escutcheons newly painted :
There in the mists beyond the peaks remainèd,
715 The day of doom four hundred thousand waited.
God ! what a grief. Franks know not what is
  fated.

LVI

Passes the day, the darkness is grown deep.
That Emperour, rich Charlès, lies asleep ;
Dreams that he stands in the great pass of Size,
720 In his two hands his ashen spear he sees ;
Guenès the count that spear from him doth seize,
Brandishes it and twists it with such ease,
That flown into the sky the flinders seem.
Charlès sleeps on nor wakens from his dream.

LVII

725 And after this another vision saw,
In France, at Aix, in his Chapelle once more,
That his right arm an evil bear did gnaw ;
Out of Ardennes he saw a leopard stalk,
His body dear did savagely assault ;
730 But then there dashed a harrier from the hall,
Leaping in the air he sped to Charlè's call,
By the right ear that felon bear he caught,
And furiously the leopard next he fought.
Of battle great the Franks then seemed to talk,
735 Yet which might win they knew not, in his
    thought.
Charlès sleeps on, nor wakens he for aught.

LVIII

Passes the night and opens the clear day ;
That Emperour canters in brave array,
Looks through the host often and everyway ;
740 " My lords barons," at length doth Charlès say,
Ye see the pass along these valleys strait,
Judge for me now, who shall in rereward wait."
" There's my good-son, Rollanz," then answers
    Guenes,
" You've no baron whose valour is so great."
745 When the King hears, he looks upon him straight,
And says to him : " You devil incarnate ;
Into your heart is come a mortal hate.
And who shall go before me in the gate ? "
" Oger is here, of Denmark ; " answers Guenes,
750 " You've no baron were better in that place."

LIX

The count Rollanz hath heard himself decreed ;
Speaks then to Guenes by rule of courtesy :
" Good-father, Sir, I ought to hold you dear,
Since the rereward you have for me decreed.
755 Charlès the King will never lose by me,
As I know well, nor charger nor palfrey,

25

Jennet nor mule that canter can with speed,
Nor sumpter-horse will lose, nor any steed ;
But my sword's point shall first exact their meed."
760 Answers him Guenes : " I know ; 'tis true indeed."

LX

When Rollant heard that he should be rerewarden
Furiously he spoke to his good-father :
" Aha ! culvert ; begotten of a bastard.
Thinkest the glove will slip from me hereafter,
765 As then from thee the wand fell before Charlès ?"

LXI

" Right Emperour," says the baron Rollanz,
" Give me the bow you carry in your hand ;
Ne'er in reproach, I know, will any man
Say that it fell from me, as Guenès chanced
770 Let fall your glove, when he received the wand."
That Emperour with lowered front doth stand,
He tugs his beard, his chin is in his hand ;
Tears fill his eyes, he cannot them command.

LXII

And after that is come duke Neimès furth,
775 (Better vassal there was not upon earth)
Says to the King : " Right well now have you
heard ;
The count Rollanz to bitter wrath is stirred,
For that on him the rereward is conferred ;
No baron else have you, would do that work.
780 Give him the bow your hands have bent, at first ;
Then find him men, his company are worth."
Gives it, the King, and Rollant bears it furth.

LXIII

That Emperour, Rollanz then calleth he :
" Fair nephew mine, know this in verity ;
785 Half of my host I leave you presently ;

26

Retain you them ; your safeguard this shall be."
Then says the count : " I will not have them, me !
Confound me God, if I fail in the deed !
Good valiant Franks, a thousand score I'll keep.
790 Go through the pass in all security,
While I'm alive there's no man you need fear."

LXIV

The count Rollanz has mounted his charger.
Beside him came his comrade Oliver,
Also Gerins and the proof count Geriers,
795 And Otès came, and also Berengiers,
Old Anséis, and Sansun too came there,
Gerart also of Rossillon the fierce,
And there is come the Gascon Engeliers.
" Now by my head I'll go ! " the Archbishop
swears.
800 " And I'm with you," says then the count Gual-
tiers,
" I'm Rollant's man, I may not leave him there."
A thousand score they choose of chevaliers.

LXV

Gualter del Hum he calls, that Count Rollanz ;
" A thousand Franks take, out of France our
land ;
805 Dispose them so, among ravines and crags,
That the Emperour lose not a single man."
Gualter replies : " I'll do as you command."
A thousand Franks, come out of France their
land,
At Gualter's word they scour ravines and crags ;
810 They'll not come down, howe'er the news be bad,
Ere from their sheaths swords seven hundred
flash.
King Almaris, Belferne for kingdom had,
On the evil day he met them in combat.

27

LXVI

High are the peaks, the valleys shadowful,
815   Swarthy the rocks, the narrows wonderful.
Franks passed that day all very sorrowful,
Fifteen leagues round the rumour of them grew.
When they were come, and Terra Major knew,
Saw Gascony their land and their seigneur's,
820   Remembering their fiefs and their honours,
Their little maids, their gentle wives and true ;
There was not one that shed not tears for rue.
Beyond the rest Charles was of anguish full,
In Spanish Pass he'd left his dear nephew ;
825   Pity him seized ; he could but weep for rue.

LXVII

The dozen peers are left behind in Spain,
Franks in their band a thousand score remain,
No fear have these, death hold they in disdain.
That Emperour goes into France apace ;
830   Under his cloke he fain would hide his face.
Up to his side comes cantering Duke Neimes,
Says to the King : " What grief upon you
     weighs ? "
Charles answers him : " He's wrong that quest-
     ion makes.
So great my grief I cannot but complain.
835   France is destroyed, by the device of Guene :
This night I saw, by an angel's vision plain,
Between my hands he brake my spear in twain ;
Great fear I have, since Rollant must remain :
I've left him there, upon a border strange.
840   God ! If he's lost, I'll not outlive that shame."

LXVIII

Charlès the great, he cannot but deplore.
And with him Franks an hundred thousand
     mourn,
Who for Rollanz have marvellous remorse.

The felon Guenes had treacherously wrought ;
845 From pagan king has had his rich reward,
Silver and gold, and veils and silken cloths,
Camels, lions, with many a mule and horse.
Barons from Spain King Marsilies hath called,
Counts and viscounts and dukes and almacours,
850 And the admirals, and cadets nobly born ;
Within three days come hundred thousands four.
In Sarraguce they sound the drums of war ;
Mahum they raise upon their highest tow'r,
Pagan is none, that does not him adore.
855 They canter then with great contention
Through Certeine land, valleys and mountains,
        on,
Till of the Franks they see the gonfalons,
Being in rereward those dozen companions ;
They will not fail battle to do anon.

LXIX

860 Marsile's nephew is come before the band,
Riding a mule, he goads it with a wand,
Smiling and clear, his uncle's ear demands :
" Fair lord and king, since, in your service, glad,
I have endured sorrow and sufferance,
865 Have fought in field, and victories have had.
Give me a fee : the right to smite Rollanz !
I'll slay him clean with my good trenchant lance,
If Mahumet will be my sure warrant ;
Spain I'll set free, deliver all her land
870 From Pass of Aspre even unto Durestant.
Charles will grow faint, and recreant the Franks ;
There'll be no war while you're a living man."
Marsilie gives the glove into his hand.

LXX

Marsile's nephew, holding in hand the glove,
875 His uncle calls, with reason proud enough :
" Fair lord and king, great gift from you I've
        won.

Choose now for me eleven more baruns,
So I may fight those dozen companions."
First before all there answers Falfarun ;
880 —Brother he was to King Marsiliun—
" Fair sir nephew, go you and I at once
Then verily this battle shall be done ;
The rereward of the great host of Carlun,
It is decreed, their death shall come from us."

LXXI

885 King Corsablis is come from the other part,
Barbarian, and steeped in evil art.
He's spoken then as fits a good vassal,
For all God's gold he would not seem coward.
Hastes into view Malprimis of Brigal,
890 Faster than a horse, upon his feet can dart,
Before Marsile he cries with all his heart :
" My body I will shew at Rencesvals ;
Find I Rollanz, I'll slay him without fault."

LXXII

An admiral is there of Balaguet ;
895 Clear face and proud, and body nobly bred ;
Since first he was upon his horse mounted,
His arms to bear has shewn great lustihead ;
In vassalage he is well famousèd ;
Christian were he, he'd shewn good baronhead.
900 Before Marsile aloud has he shouted :
" To Rencesvals my body shall be led ;
Find I Rollanz, then is he surely dead,
And Oliver, and all the dozen else ;
Franks shall be slain in grief and wretchedness.
905 Charlès the great is old now and doted,
Weary will be and make no war again ;
Spain shall be ours, in peace and quietness."
King Marsilies has heard, and thanks him well.

LXXIII

An almacour is there of Moriane,
More felon none in all the land of Spain.
Before Marsile his vaunting boast hath made :
" To Rencesvals my company I'll take,
A thousand score, with shields and lances brave.
Find I Rollanz, with death I'll him acquaint ;
Day shall not dawn but Charles will make his
    plaint."

LXXIV

From the other part, Turgis of Turtelose,
He was a count, that city was his own ;
Christians he would them massacre, every one.
Before Marsile among the rest is gone,
Says to the King : " Let not dismay be shewn !
Mahum's more worth than Saint Peter of Rome ;
Serve we him well, then fame in field we'll own.
To Rencesvals, to meet Rollanz I'll go,
From death he'll find his warranty in none.
See here my sword, that is both good and long
With Durendal I'll lay it well across ;
Ye'll hear betimes to which the prize is gone.
Franks shall be slain, whom we descend upon,
Charlès the old will suffer grief and wrong,
No more on earth his crown will he put on."

LXXV

From the other part, Escremiz of Valtrenne,
A Sarrazin, that land was his as well.
Before Marsile he cries amid the press :
To Rencesvals I go, pride to make less ;
Find I Rollanz, he'll not bear thence his head,
Nor Oliver that hath the others led,
The dozen peers condemnèd are to death ;
Franks shall be slain, and France lie deserted.
Of good vassals will Charles be richly bled."

940 From the other part, a pagan Esturganz ;
Estramariz also, was his comrade ;
Felons were these, and traitors miscreant.
Then said Marsile : " My Lords, before me
stand !
Into the pass ye'll go to Rencesvals,
945 Give me your aid, and thither lead my band."
They answer him : " Sire, ev'n as you com-
mand.
We will assault Olivier and Rollant,
The dozen peers from death have no warrant ;
For these our swords are trusty and trenchant,
950 In scalding blood we'll dye their blades scarlat.
Franks shall be slain, and Charlès be right sad.
Terra Major we'll give into your hand ;
Come there, Sir king, truly you'll see all that ;
Yea, the Emperour we'll give into your hand."

LXXVII

955 Running there came Margariz of Sibile,
Who holds the land by Cadiz, to the sea.
For his beauty the ladies hold him dear ;
Who looks on him, with him her heart is pleased,
When she beholds, she can but smile for glee.
960 Was no pagan of such high chivalry.
Comes through the press, above them all cries he,
" Be not at all dismayed, king Marsilie !
To Rencesvals I go, and Rollanz, he
Nor Oliver may scape alive from me ;
965 The dozen peers are doomed to martyry.
See here the sword, whose hilt is gold indeed,
I got in gift from the admiral of Primes ;
In scarlat blood I pledge it shall be steeped.
Franks shall be slain, and France abasèd be.
970 To Charles the old, with his great blossoming
beard,
Day shall not dawn but brings him rage and grief,
Ere a year pass, all France we shall have seized,

Till we can lie in th' burgh of Saint Denise."
The pagan king has bowed his head down deep.

LXXVIII

975 From the other part, Chernublès of Muneigre.
Right to the ground his hair swept either way ;
He for a jest would bear a heavier weight
Than four yoked mules, beneath their load that
strain.
That land he had, God's curse on it was plain.
980 No sun shone there, nor grew there any grain,
No dew fell there, nor any shower of rain,
The very stones were black upon that plain ;
And many say that devils there remain.
Says Chernublès : " My sword is in its place,
985 At Rencesvals scarlat I will it stain ;
Find I Rollanz the proud upon my way,
I'll fall on him, or trust me not again,
And Durendal I'll conquer with this blade,
Franks shall be slain, and France a desert made."
990 The dozen peers are, at this word, away,
Five score thousand of Sarrazins they take ;
Who keenly press, and on to battle haste ;
In a fir-wood their gear they ready make.

LXXIX

Ready they make hauberks Sarrazinese,
995 That folded are, the greater part, in three ;
And they lace on good helms Sarragucese ;
Gird on their swords of tried steel Viennese ;
Fine shields they have, and spears Valentinese,
And white, blue, red, their ensigns take the
breeze,
1000 They've left their mules behind, and their pal-
freys,
Their chargers mount, and canter knee by knee.
Fair shines the sun, the day is bright and clear,
Light burns again from all their polished gear.

A thousand horns they sound, more proud to
    seem ;
1005 Great is the noise, the Franks its echo hear.
Says Oliver : " Companion, I believe,
Sarrazins now in battle must we meet."
Answers Rollanz : " God grant us then the fee !
For our King's sake well must we quit us here ;
1010 Man for his lord should suffer great disease,
Most bitter cold endure, and burning heat,
His hair and skin should offer up at need.
Now must we each lay on most hardily,
So evil songs ne'er sung of us shall be.
1015 Pagans are wrong : Christians are right indeed.
Evil example will never come of me."

LXXX

Oliver mounts upon a lofty peak,
Looks to his right along the valley green,
The pagan tribes approaching there appear ;
1020 He calls Rollanz, his companion, to see :
" What sound is this, come out of Spain, we hear,
What hauberks bright, what helmets these that
    gleam ?
They'll smite our Franks with fury past belief,
He knew it, Guenes, the traitor and the thief,
1025 Who chose us out before the King our chief."
Answers the count Rollanz : " Olivier, cease.
That man is my good-father ; hold thy peace.'

LXXXI

Upon a peak is Oliver mounted,
Kingdom of Spain he sees before him spread,
1030 And Sarrazins, so many gatherèd.
Their helmets gleam, with gold are jewellèd,
Also their shields, their hauberks orfreyèd,
Also their swords, ensigns on spears fixèd.
Rank beyond rank could not be numberèd,
1035 So many there, no measure could he set.
In his own heart he's sore astonishèd,

Fast as he could, down from the peak hath sped,
Comes to the Franks, to them his tale hath said.

LXXXII

Says Oliver : " Pagans from there I saw ;
1040 Never on earth did any man see more.
Gainst us their shields an hundred thousand
    bore,
That lacèd helms and shining hauberks wore ;
And, bolt upright, their bright brown spearheads
    shone.
Battle we'll have as never was before.
1045 Lords of the Franks, God keep you in valour !
So hold your ground, we be not overborne ! "
Then say the Franks : " Shame take him that
    goes off :
If we must die, then perish one and all."

LXXXIII

Says Oliver : " Pagans in force abound,
1050 While of us Franks but very few I count ;
Comrade Rollanz, your horn I pray you sound !
If Charlès hear, he'll turn his armies round."
Answers Rollanz : " A fool I should be found ;
In France the Douce would perish my renown.
1055 With Durendal I'll lay on thick and stout,
In blood the blade, to its golden hilt, I'll drown.
Felon pagans to th' pass shall not come down ;
I pledge you now, to death they all are bound."

LXXXIV

" Comrade Rollanz, sound the olifant, I pray ;
1060 If Charlès hear, the host he'll turn again ;
Will succour us our King and baronage."
Answers Rollanz : " Never, by God, I say,
For my misdeed shall kinsmen hear the blame,
Nor France the Douce fall into evil fame !
1065 Rather stout blows with Durendal I'll lay,

35

With my good sword that by my side doth sway ;
Till bloodied o'er you shall behold the blade.
Felon pagans are gathered to their shame ;
I pledge you now, to death they're doomed to-
day."

LXXXV

1070 " Comrade Rollanz, once sound your olifant !
If Charlès hear, where in the pass he stands,
I pledge you now, they'll turn again, the Franks."
" Never, by God," then answers him Rollanz,
" Shall it be said by any living man,
1075 That for pagans I took my horn in hand !
Never by me shall men reproach my clan.
When I am come into the battle grand,
And blows lay on, by hundred, by thousand,
Of Durendal bloodied you'll see the brand.
1080 Franks are good men ; like vassals brave they'll
stand ;
Nay, Spanish men from death have no warrant."

LXXXVI

Says Oliver : " In this I see no blame ;
I have beheld the Sarrazins of Spain ;
Covered with them, the mountains and the vales,
1085 The wastes I saw, and all the farthest plains.
A muster great they've made, this people strange;
We have of men a very little tale."
Answers Rollanz : " My anger is inflamed.
Never, please God His Angels and His Saints,
1090 Never by me shall Frankish valour fail !
Rather I'll die than shame shall me attain.
Therefore strike on, the Emperour's love to
gain."

LXXXVII

Pride hath Rollanz, wisdom Olivier hath ;
And both of them shew marvellous courage ;
1095 Once they are horsed, once they have donned
their arms,

36

Rather they'ld die than from the battle pass.
Good are the counts, and lofty their language.
Felon pagans come cantering in their wrath.
Says Oliver : " Behold and see, Rollanz,
1100 These are right near, but Charles is very far.
On the olifant deign now to sound a blast ;
Were the King here, we should not fear damage.
Only look up towards the Pass of Aspre,
In sorrow there you'll see the whole rereward.
1105 Who does this deed, does no more afterward."
Answers Rollanz : " Utter not such outrage !
Evil his heart that is in thought coward !
We shall remain firm in our place installed ;
From us the blows shall come, from us the assault."

LXXXVIII

1110 When Rollant sees that now must be combat,
More fierce he's found than lion or leopard ;
The Franks he calls, and Oliver commands :
" Now say no more, my friends, nor thou, com-
        rade.
That Emperour, who left us Franks on guard,
1115 A thousand score stout men he set apart,
And well he knows, not one will prove coward.
Man for his lord should suffer with good heart,
Of bitter cold and great heat bear the smart,
His blood let drain, and all his flesh be scarred.
1120 Strike with thy lance, and I with Durendal,
With my good sword that was the King's reward.
So, if I die, who has it afterward
Noble vassal's he well may say it was."

LXXXIX

From the other part is the Archbishop Turpin,
1125 He pricks his horse and mounts upon a hill ;
Calling the Franks, sermon to them begins :
" My lords barons, Charles left us here for this ;
He is our King, well may we die for him :
To Christendom good service offering.

37

1130 Battle you'll have, you all are bound to it,
For with your eyes you see the Sarrazins.
Pray for God's grace, confessing Him your sins !
For your souls' health, I'll absolution give ;
So, though you die, blest martyrs shall you live,
1135 Thrones you shall win in the great Paradis."
The Franks dismount, upon the ground are lit.
That Archbishop God's Benediction gives,
For their penance, good blows to strike he bids.

XC

The Franks arise, and stand upon their feet,
1140 They're well absolved, and from their sins made
clean,
And the Archbishop has signed them with God's
seal ;
And next they mount upon their chargers keen ;
By rule of knights they have put on their gear,
For battle all apparelled as is meet.
1145 The count Rollanz calls Oliver, and speaks :
" Comrade and friend, now clearly have you
seen
That Guenelun hath got us by deceit ;
Gold hath he ta'en ; much wealth is his to keep ;
That Emperour vengeance for us must wreak.
1150 King Marsilies hath bargained for us cheap ;
At the sword's point he yet shall pay our meed."

XCI

To Spanish pass is Rollanz now going
On Veillantif, his good steed, galloping ;
He is well armed, pride is in his bearing,
1155 He goes, so brave, his spear in hand holding,
He goes, its point against the sky turning ;
A gonfalon all white thereon he's pinned,
Down to his hand flutters the golden fringe :
Noble his limbs, his face clear and smiling.
1160 His companion goes after, following,
The men of France their warrant find in him.

Proudly he looks towards the Sarrazins,
And to the Franks sweetly, himself humbling ;
And courteously has said to them this thing :
1165 " My lords barons, go now your pace holding !
Pagans are come great martyrdom seeking ;
Noble and fair reward this day shall bring,
Was never won by any Frankish King."
Upon these words the hosts are come touching.

XCII

1170 Speaks Oliver : " No more now will I say.
Your olifant, to sound it do not deign,
Since from Carlun you'll never more have aid.
He has not heard ; no fault of his, so brave.
Those with him there are never to be blamed.
1175 So canter on, with what prowess you may !
Lords and barons, firmly your ground maintain !
Be minded well, I pray you in God's Name,
Stout blows to strike, to give as you shall take.
Forget the cry of Charles we never may."
1180 Upon this word the Franks cry out amain.
Who then had heard them all " Monjoie ! "
    acclaim
Of vassalage might well recall the tale.
They canter forth, God ! with what proud parade,
Pricking their spurs, the better speed to gain ;
1185 They go to strike,—what other thing could they?—
But Sarrazins are not at all afraid.
Pagans and Franks, you'ld see them now engaged.

XCIII

Marsile's nephew, his name is Aëlroth,
First of them all canters before the host,
1190 Says of our Franks these ill words as he goes :
" Felons of France, so here on us you close !
Betrayed you has he that to guard you ought ;
Mad is the King who left you in this post.
So shall the fame of France the Douce be lost,
1195 And the right arm from Charlè's body torn."

When Rollant hears, what rage he has, by God
His steed he spurs, gallops with great effort ;
He goes, that count, to strike with all his force,
The shield he breaks, the hauberk's seam unsews,
1200 Slices the heart, and shatters up the bones,
All of the spine he severs with that blow,
And with his spear the soul from body throws
So well he's pinned, he shakes in the air that
        corse,
On his spear's hilt he's flung it from the horse :
1205 So in two halves Aëlroth's neck he broke,
Nor left him yet, they say, but rather spoke :
" Avaunt, culvert ! A madman Charles is not,
No treachery was ever in his thought.
Proudly he did, who left us in this post ;
1210 The fame of France the Douce shall not be lost.
Strike on, the Franks ! Ours are the foremost
        blows.
For we are right, but these gluttons are wrong."

XCIV

A duke there was, his name was Falfarun,
Brother was he to King Marsiliun,
1215 He held their land, Dathan's and Abirun's ;
Beneath the sky no more encrimed felun ;
Between his eyes so broad was he in front
A great half-foot you'ld measure there in full.
His nephew dead he's seen with grief enough,
1220 Comes through the press and wildly forth he
        runs,
Aloud he shouts their cry the pagans use ;
And to the Franks is right contrarious :
" Honour of France the Douce shall fall to us ! "
Hears Oliver, he's very furious,
1225 His horse he pricks with both his golden spurs,
And goes to strike, ev'n as a baron doth ;
The shield he breaks and through the hauberk
        cuts,
His ensign's fringe into the carcass thrusts,

On his spear's hilt he's flung it dead in dust.

1230 Looks on the ground, sees glutton lying thus,
And says to him, with reason proud enough :
" From threatening, culvert, your mouth I've
    shut.
Strike on, the Franks ! Right well we'll over-
    come."
" Monjoie," he shouts, 'twas the ensign of Carlun.

XCV

1235 A king there was, his name was Corsablix,
Barbarian, and of a strange country,
He's called aloud to the other Sarrazins :
" Well may we join battle upon this field,
For of the Franks but very few are here ;
1240 And those are here, we should account them
    cheap,
From Charles not one has any warranty.
This is the day when they their death shall meet."
Has heard him well that Archbishop Turpin,
No man he'ld hate so much the sky beneath ;
1245 Spurs of fine gold he pricks into his steed,
To strike that king by virtue great goes he,
The hauberk all unfastens, breaks the shield,
Thrusts his great spear in through the carcass
    clean,
Pins it so well he shakes it in its seat,
1250 Dead in the road he's flung it from his spear.
Looks on the ground, that glutton lying sees,
Nor leaves him yet, they say, but rather speaks :
" Culvert pagan, you lied now in your teeth,
Charlès my lord our warrant is indeed ;
1255 None of our Franks hath any mind to flee.
Your companions all on this spot we'll keep,
I tell you news ; death shall ye suffer here.
Strike on, the Franks ! Fail none of you at need !
Ours the first blow, to God the glory be ! "
1260 " Monjoie ! " he cries, for all the camp to hear.

41

XCVI

And Gerins strikes Malprimis of Brigal
So his good shield is nothing worth at all,
Shatters the boss, was fashioned of crystal,
One half of it downward to earth flies off ;
1265   Right to the flesh has through his hauberk torn,
On his good spear he has the carcass caught.
And with one blow that pagan downward falls ;
The soul of him Satan away hath borne.

XCVII

And his comrade Gerers strikes the admiral,
1270   The shield he breaks, the hauberk unmetals,
And his good spear drives into his vitals,
So well he's pinned him, clean through the
    carcass,
Dead on the field he's flung him from his hand.
Says Oliver : " Now is our battle grand."

XCVIII

1275   Sansun the Duke goes strike that almacour,   ,
The shield he breaks, with golden flowers tooled
That good hauberk for him is nothing proof,
He's sliced the heart, the lungs and liver through,
And flung him dead, as well or ill may prove.
1280   Says the Archbishop : " A baron's stroke, in
    truth."

XCIX

And Anséis has let his charger run ;
He goes to strike Turgis of Turtelus,
The shield he breaks, its golden boss above,
The hauberk too, its doubled mail undoes,
1285   His good spear's point into the carcass runs,
So well he's thrust, clean through the whole steel
    comes,
And from the hilt he's thrown him dead in dust.
Then says Rollant : " Great prowess in that
    thrust."

C

And Engelers the Gascoin of Burdele
1290 Spurs on his horse, lets fall the reins as well,
He goes to strike Escremiz of Valtrene,
The shield he breaks and shatters on his neck,
The hauberk too, he has its chinguard rent,
Between the arm-pits has pierced him through
    the breast,
1295 On his spear's hilt from saddle throws him dead ;
After he says : " So are you turned to hell."

CI

And Otès strikes a pagan Estorgant
Upon the shield, before its leathern band,
Slices it through, the white with the scarlat ;
1300 The hauberk too, has torn its folds apart,
And his good spear thrusts clean through the
    carcass,
And flings it dead, ev'n as the horse goes past ;
He says : " You have no warrant afterward."

CII

And Berenger, he strikes Estramariz,
1305 The shield he breaks, the hauberk tears and
    splits,
Thrusts his stout spear through's middle, and
    him flings
Down dead among a thousand Sarrazins.
Of their dozen peers ten have now been killed,
No more than two remain alive and quick,
1310 Being Chernuble, and the count Margariz.

CIII

Margariz is a very gallant knight,
Both fair and strong, and swift he is and light ;
He spurs his horse, goes Oliver to strike,
And breaks his shield, by th'golden buckle
    bright ;

1315 Along his ribs the pagan's spear doth glide ;
God's his warrant, his body has respite,
The shaft breaks off, Oliver stays upright ;
That other goes, naught stays him in his flight,
His trumpet sounds, rallies his tribe to fight.

CIV

1320 Common the fight is now and marvellous.
The count Rollanz no way himself secures,
Strikes with his spear, long as the shaft endures,
By fifteen blows it is clean broken through ;
Then Durendal he bares, his sabre good
1325 Spurs on his horse, is gone to strike Chernuble,
The helmet breaks, where bright carbuncles
grew,
Slices the cap and shears the locks in two,
Slices also the eyes and the features,
The hauberk white, whose mail was close of woof,
1330 Down to the groin cuts all his body through
To the saddle ; with beaten gold 'twas tooled.
Upon the horse that sword a moment stood,
Then sliced its spine, no join there any knew,
Dead in the field among thick grass them threw.
1335 After he said : " Culvert, false step you moved,
From Mahumet your help will not come soon.
No victory for gluttons such as you."

CV

The count Rollanz, he canters through the field,
Holds Durendal, he well can thrust and wield,
1340 Right great damage he's done the Sarrazines
You'd seen them, one on other, dead in heaps,
Through all that place their blood was flowing
clear !
In blood his arms were and his hauberk steeped,
And bloodied o'er, shoulders and neck, his steed.
1345 And Oliver goes on to strike with speed ;
No blame that way deserve the dozen peers,
For all the Franks they strike and slay with heat,

44

Pagans are slain, some swoon there in their seats,
Says the Archbishop : " Good baronage indeed ! "
1350 " Monjoie " he cries, the call of Charles repeats.

CVI

And Oliver has cantered through the crush ;
Broken his spear, the truncheon still he thrusts ;
Going to strike a pagan Malsarun ;
Flowers and gold, are on the shield, he cuts,
1355 Out of the head both the two eyes have burst,
And all the brains are fallen in the dust ;
He flings him dead, sev'n hundred else amongst.
Then has he slain Turgin and Esturgus ;
Right to the hilt, his spear in flinders flew.
1360 Then says Rollant : " Companion, what do you?
In such a fight, there's little strength in wood,
Iron and steel should here their valour prove.
Where is your sword, that Halteclere I knew ?
Golden its hilt, whereon a crystal grew."
1365 Says Oliver : " I had not, if I drew,
Time left to strike enough good blows and true."

CVII

Then Oliver has drawn his mighty sword
As his comrade had bidden and implored,
In knightly wise the blade to him has shewed ;
1370 Justin he strikes, that Iron Valley's lord,
All of his head has down the middle shorn,
The carcass sliced, the broidered sark has torn,
The good saddle that was with gold adorned,
And through the spine has sliced that pagan's
        horse ;
1375 Dead in the field before his feet they fall.
" Now," says Rollanz : " my brother I you call ;
He'll love us for such blows, our Emperor."
On every side " Monjoie " you'ld hear them
        roar.

45

CVIII

That count Gerins sate on his horse Sorel,
1380 On Passe-Cerf was Gerers there, his friend ;
They've loosed their reins, together spurred
and sped,
And go to strike a pagan Timozel ;
One on the shield, on hauberk the other fell ;
And their two spears went through the carcass
well,
1385 A fallow field amidst they've thrown him dead.
I do not know, I never heard it said
Which of the two was nimbler as they went.
Esperveris was there, son of Borel,
And him there slew Engelers of Burdel.
1390 And the Archbishop, he slew them Siglorel,
The enchanter, who before had been in hell,
Where Jupiter bore him by a magic spell.
Then Turpin says : " To us he's forfeited."
Answers Rollanz : " The culvert is bested.
1395 Such blows, brother Olivier, I like well."

CIX

The battle grows more hard and harder yet,
Franks and pagans, with marvellous onset,
Each other strike and each himself defends.
So many shafts bloodstained and shatterèd,
1400 So many flags and ensigns tatterèd ;
So many Franks lose their young lustihead,
Who'll see no more their mothers nor their
friends,
Nor hosts of France, that in the pass attend.
Charlès the Great weeps therefor with regret.
1405 What profits that ? No succour shall they get.
Evil service, that day, Guenes rendered them,
To Sarraguce going, his own to sell.
After he lost his members and his head,
In court, at Aix, to gallows-tree condemned ;
1410 And thirty more with him, of his kindred,
Were hanged, a thing they never did expect.

CX

Now marvellous and weighty the combat,
Right well they strike, Olivier and Rollant,
A thousand blows come from the Archbishop's
    hand,
1415 The dozen peers are nothing short of that,
With one accord join battle all the Franks.
Pagans are slain by hundred, by thousand,
Who flies not then, from death has no warrant,
Will he or nill, foregoes the allotted span.
1420 The Franks have lost the foremost of their band,
They'll see no more their fathers nor their clans,
Nor Charlemagne, where in the pass he stands.
Torment arose, right marvellous, in France,
Tempest there was, of wind and thunder black,
1425 With rain and hail, so much could not be spanned;
Fell thunderbolts often on every hand,
And verily the earth quaked in answer back
From Saint Michael of Peril unto Sanz,
From Besençun to the harbour of Guitsand ;
1430 No house stood there but straight its walls must
    crack :
In full mid-day the darkness was so grand,
Save the sky split, no light was in the land.
Beheld these things with terror every man,
And many said : " We in the Judgement stand ;
1435 The end of time is presently at hand."
They spake no truth ; they did not understand ;
'Twas the great day of mourning for Rollant.

CXI

The Franks strike on ; their hearts are good and
    stout.
Pagans are slain, a thousandfold, in crowds,
1440 Left of five score are not two thousands now.
Says the Archbishop : " Our men are very proud,
No man on earth has more nor better found.
In Chronicles of Franks is written down,
What vassalage he had, our Emperour."

47

1445 Then through the field they go, their friends
  seek out,
And their eyes weep with grief and pain profound
For kinsmen dear, by hearty friendship bound.
King Marsilies and his great host draw round.

CXII

King Marsilies along a valley led
1450 The mighty host that he had gatherèd.
Twenty columns that king had numberèd.
With gleaming gold their helms were jewellèd.
Shone too their shields and sarks embroiderèd.
Sounded the charge seven thousand trumpets,
1455 Great was the noise through all that country
  went.
Then said Rollanz : " Olivier, brother, friend,
That felon Guenes hath sworn to achieve our
  death ;
For his treason no longer is secret.
Right great vengeance our Emperour will get.
1460 Battle we'll have, both long and keenly set,
Never has man beheld such armies met.
With Durendal my sword I'll strike again,
And, comrade, you shall strike with Halteclere.
These swords in lands so many have we held,
1465 Battles with them so many brought to end,
No evil song shall e'er be sung or said."

CXIII

When the Franks see so many there, pagans,
On every side covering all the land,
Often they call Olivier and Rollant,
1470 The dozen peers, to be their safe warrant.
And the Archbishop speaks to them, as he can :
" My lords barons, go thinking nothing bad !
For God I pray you fly not hence but stand,
Lest evil songs of our valour men chant !
1475 Far better 't were to perish in the van.
Certain it is, our end is near at hand,

Beyond this day shall no more live one man ;
But of one thing I give you good warrant :
Blest Paradise to you now open stands,
1480 By the Innocents your thrones you there shall
  have."
Upon these words grow bold again the Franks ;
There is not one but he " Monjoie " demands.

CXIV

A Sarrazin was there, of Sarraguce,
Of that city one half was his by use,
1485 'Twas Climborins, a man was nothing proof ;
By Guenelun the count an oath he took,
And kissed his mouth in amity and truth,
Gave him his sword and his carbuncle too.
Terra Major, he said, to shame he'ld put,
1490 From the Emperour his crown he would remove.
He sate his horse, which he called Barbamusche,
Never so swift sparrow nor swallow flew,.
He spurred him well, and down the reins he
  threw,
Going to strike Engelier of Gascune ;
1495 Nor shield nor sark him any warrant proved,
The pagan spear's point did his body wound,
He pinned him well, and all the steel sent through,
From the hilt flung him dead beneath his foot.
After he said : " Good are they to confuse.
1500 Pagans, strike on, and so this press set loose ! "
" God ! " say the Franks, " Grief, such a man
  to lose ! "

CXV

The count Rollanz called upon Oliver :
" Sir companion, dead now is Engeler ;
Than whom we'd no more valiant chevalier."
1505 Answered that count : " God, let me him
  avenge ! "
Spurs of fine gold into his horse drove then,

49

Held Halteclere, with blood its steel was red,
By virtue great to strike that pagan went,
Brandished his blade, the Sarrazin upset ;
1510   The Adversaries of God his soul bare thence.
Next he has slain the duke Alphaïen,
And sliced away Escababi his head,
And has unhorsed some seven Arabs else ;
No good for those to go to war again.
1515   Then said Rollanz : " My comrade shews anger,
So in my sight he makes me prize him well ;
More dear by Charles for such blows are we
        held."
Aloud he's cried : " Strike on, the chevaliers !"

CXVI

From the other part a pagan Valdabron.
1520   Warden he'd been to king Marsilion,
And lord, by sea, of four hundred dromonds ;
No sailor was but called his name upon ;
Jerusalem he'd taken by treason,
Violated the Temple of Salomon,
1525   The Patriarch had slain before the fonts.
He'd pledged his oath by county Guenelon,
Gave him his sword, a thousand coins thereon.
He sate his horse, which he called Gramimond,
Never so swift flew in the air falcon ;
1530   He's pricked him well, with sharp spurs he had
        on,
Going to strike e'en that rich Duke, Sanson ;
His shield has split, his hauberk has undone,
The ensign's folds have through his body gone,
Dead from the hilt out of his seat he's dropt :
1535   " Pagans, strike on, for well we'll overcome ! "
" God ! " say the Franks, " Grief for a brave
        baron ! "

CXVII

The count Rollanz, when Sansun dead he saw,
You may believe, great grief he had therefor.

His horse he spurs, gallops with great effort,
1540 Wields Durendal, was worth fine gold and more,
Goes as he may to strike that baron bold
Above the helm, that was embossed with gold,
Slices the head, the sark, and all the corse,
The good saddle, that was embossed with gold,
1545 And cuts deep through the backbone of his
    horse ;
He's slain them both, blame him for that or laud.
The pagans say : " 'Twas hard on us, that blow."
Answers Rollanz : " Nay, love you I can not,
For on your side is arrogance and wrong."

CXVIII

1550 Out of Affrike an Affrican was come,
'Twas Malquiant, the son of king Malcud ;
With beaten gold was all his armour done,
Fore all men's else it shone beneath the sun.
He sate his horse, which he called Salt-Perdut,
1555 Never so swift was any beast could run.
And Anséis upon the shield he struck,
The scarlat with the blue he sliced it up,
Of his hauberk he's torn the folds and cut,
The steel and stock has through his body thrust.
1560 Dead is that count, he's no more time to run.
Then say the Franks : " Baron, an evil luck ! "

CXIX

Swift through the field Turpin the Archbishop
    passed ;
Such shaven-crown has never else sung Mass
Who with his limbs such prowess might com-
    pass ;
1565 To th'pagan said : " God send thee all that's
    bad !
One thou hast slain for whom my heart is sad."
So his good horse forth at his bidding ran,
He's struck him then on his shield Toledan,
Until he flings him dead on the green grass.

51

CXX

1570 From the other part was a pagan Grandones,
Son of Capuel, the king of Capadoce.
He sate his horse, the which he called Marmore,
Never so swift was any bird in course ;
He's loosed the reins, and spurring on that horse
1575 He's gone to strike Gerin with all his force ;
The scarlat shield from's neck he's broken off,
And all his sark thereafter has he torn,
The ensign blue clean through his body's gone,
Until he flings him dead, on a high rock ;
1580 His companion Gerer he's slain also,
And Berenger, and Guiun of Santone ;
Next a rich duke he's gone to strike, Austore,
That held Valence and the Honour of the Rhone;
He's flung him dead ; great joy the pagans shew.
1585 Then say the Franks : " Of ours how many fall."

CXXI

The count Rollanz, his sword with blood is
stained,
Well has he heard what way the Franks com-
plained ;
Such grief he has, his heart would split in twain :
To the pagan says : " God send thee every
shame !
1590 One hast thou slain whom dearly thou'lt repay."
He spurs his horse, that on with speed doth strain;
Which should forfeit, they both together came.

CXXII

Grandonie was both proof and valiant,
And virtuous, a vassal combatant.
1595 Upon the way there, he has met Rollant ;
He'd never seen, yet knew him at a glance,
By the proud face and those fine limbs he had,
By his regard, and by his contenance ;
He could not help but he grew faint thereat,

52

1600 He would escape, nothing avail he can.
Struck him the count, with so great virtue, that
To the nose-plate he's all the helmet cracked,
Sliced through the nose and mouth and teeth he
has,
Hauberk close-mailed, and all the whole carcass,
1605 Saddle of gold, with plates of silver flanked,
And of his horse has deeply scarred the back ;
He's slain them both, they'll make no more
attack :
The Spanish men in sorrow cry, " Alack ! "
Then say the Franks : " He strikes well, our
warrant."

CXXIII

1610 Marvellous is the battle in its speed,
The Franks there strike with vigour and with
heat,
Cutting through wrists and ribs and chines in-
deed,
Through garments to the lively flesh beneath ;
On the green grass the clear blood runs in
streams.
1615 The pagans say : " No more we'll suffer, we.
Terra Major, Mahummet's curse on thee !
Beyond all men thy people are hardy ! "
There was not one but cried then : " Marsilie,
Canter, o king, thy succour now we need ! "

CXXIV

1620 Marvellous is the battle now and grand,
The Franks there strike, their good brown spears
in hand.
Then had you seen such sorrowing of clans,
So many a slain, shattered and bleeding man !
Biting the earth, or piled there on their backs !
1625 The Sarrazins cannot such loss withstand.
Will they or nill, from off the field draw back ;
By lively force chase them away the Franks.

Their martyrdom, his men's, Marsile has seen,
So he bids sound his horns and his buccines ;
1630 Then canters forth with all his great army.
Canters before a Sarrazin, Abisme,
More felon none was in that company ;
Cankered with guile and every felony ,
He fears not God, the Son of Saint Mary ;
1635 Black is that man as molten pitch that seethes ;
Better he loves murder and treachery
Than to have all the gold of Galicie ;
Never has man beheld him sport for glee ;
Yet vassalage he's shown, and great folly,
1640 So is he dear to th' felon king Marsile ;
Dragon he bears, to which his tribe rally.
That Archbishop could never love him, he ;
Seeing him there, to strike he's very keen,
Within himself he says all quietly :
1645 " This Sarrazin great heretick meseems,
Rather I'ld die, than not go slay him clean,
Ne'er did I love coward nor cowardice."

CXXVI

That Archbishop begins the fight again,
Sitting the horse which he took from Grossaille ;
1650 —That was a king he had in Denmark slain ;—
That charger is swift and of noble race ;
Fine are his hooves, his legs are smooth and
   straight,
Short are his thighs, broad crupper he displays,
Long are his ribs, aloft his spine is raised,
1655 White is his tail and yellow is his mane,
Little his ears, and tawny all his face ;
No beast is there, can match him in a race.
That Archbishop spurs on by vassalage,
He will not pause ere Abisme he assail ;
1660 So strikes that shield, is wonderfully arrayed,
Whereon are stones, amethyst and topaze,
Esterminals and carbuncles that blaze ;

A devil's gift it was, in Val Metase,
Who handed it to the admiral Galafes ;
1665 So Turpin strikes, spares him not anyway ;
After that blow, he's worth no penny wage ;
The carcass he's sliced, rib from rib away,
So flings him down dead in an empty place.
Then say the Franks : " He has great vassal-
age,
1670 With the Archbishop, surely the Cross is safe."

CXXVII

The count Rollanz calls upon Oliver :
" Sir companion, witness you'll freely bear,
The Archbishop is a right good chevalier,
None better goes neath Heaven anywhere ;
1675 Well can he strike with lance and well with spear."
Answers that count : " Support to him we'll
bear ! "
Upon that word the Franks again make yare ;
Hard are the blows, slaughter and suffering
there,
For Christians too, most bitter grief and care.
1680 Who could had seen Rollanz and Oliver
With their good swords to strike and to slaughter !
And the Archbishop lays on there with his spear.
Those that are dead, men well may hold them
dear.
In charters and in briefs is written clear,
1685 Four thousand fell, and more, the tales declare.
Gainst four assaults easily did they fare,
But then the fifth brought heavy griefs to bear.
They all are slain, those Frankish chevaliers ;
Only three-score, whom God was pleased to
spare,
1690 Before these die, they'll sell them very dear.

CXXVIII

The count Rollanz great loss of his men sees,
His companion Olivier calls, and speaks :

55

" Sir and comrade, in God's Name, That you
    keeps,
Such good vassals you see lie here in heaps ;
1695   For France the Douce, fair country, may we
    weep,
Of such barons long desolate she'll be.
Ah ! King and friend, wherefore are you not
    here ?
How, Oliver, brother, can we achieve ?
And by what means our news to him repeat ? "
1700   Says Oliver : " I know not how to seek ;
Rather I'ld die than shame come of this feat."

CXXIX

Then says Rollanz : " I'll wind this olifant,
If Charlès hear, where in the pass he stands,
I pledge you now they will return, the Franks."
1705   Says Oliver : " Great shame would come of
    that ;
And a reproach on every one, your clan,
That shall endure while each lives in the land,
When I implored, you would not do this act ;
Doing it now, no praise from me you'll have :
1710   So wind your horn, but not by courage rash,
Seeing that both your arms with blood are
    splashed."
Answers that count : " Fine blows I've struck
    them back."

CXXX

Then says Rollant : " Strong is it now, our battle;
I'll wind my horn, so the King hears it, Charlès."
1715   Says Oliver : " That act were not a vassal's.
When I implored you, comrade, you were wrath-
    ful.
Were the King here, we had not borne such
    damage.
Nor should we blame those with him there, his
    army."

Says Oliver : " Now by my beard, hereafter
1720   If I may see my gentle sister Alde,
She in her arms, I swear, shall never clasp you."

CXXXI

Then says Rollanz : " Wherefore so wroth with
    me ? "
He answers him : " Comrade, it was your deed :
Vassalage comes by sense, and not folly ;
1725   Prudence more worth is than stupidity.
Here are Franks dead, all for your trickery ;
No service more to Carlun may we yield.
My lord were here now, had you trusted me,
And fought and won this battle then had we,
1730   Taken or slain were the king Marsilie.
In your prowess, Rollanz, no good we've seen !
Charlès the great in vain your aid will seek—
None such as he till God His Judgement speak;—
Here must you die, and France in shame be
    steeped ;
1735   Here perishes our loyal company,
Before this night great severance and grief."

CXXXII

That Archbishop has heard them, how they spoke,
His horse he pricks with his fine spurs of gold,
Coming to them he takes up his reproach :
1740   " Sir Oliver, and you, Sir Rollant, both,
For God I pray, do not each other scold !
No help it were to us, the horn to blow,
But, none the less, it may be better so ;
The King will come, with vengeance that he
    owes ;
1745   These Spanish men never away shall go.
Our Franks here, each descending from his
    horse,
Will find us dead, and limb from body torn ;
They'll take us hence, on biers and litters borne ;
With pity and with grief for us they'll mourn ;

57

1750 They'll bury each in some old minster-close;
No wolf nor swine nor dog shall gnaw our bones."
Answers Rollant: " Sir, very well you spoke."

CXXXIII

Rollant hath set the olifant to his mouth,
He grasps it well, and with great virtue sounds.
1755 High are those peaks, afar it rings and loud,
Thirty great leagues they hear its echoes mount.
So Charlès heard, and all his comrades round;
Then said that King: " Battle they do, our
      counts."
And Guenelun answered, contrarious:
1760 " That were a lie, in any other mouth."

CXXXIV

The Count Rollanz, with sorrow and with pangs,
And with great pain sounded his olifant:
Out of his mouth the clear blood leaped and ran,
About his brain the very temples cracked.
1765 Loud is its voice, that horn he holds in hand;
Charlès hath heard, where in the pass he stands,
And Neimès hears, and listen all the Franks.
Then says the King: " I hear his horn, Rollant's;
He'd never sound, but he were in combat."
1770 Answers him Guenes: " It is no battle, that.
Now are you old, blossoming white and blanched,
Yet by such words you still appear infant.
You know full well the great pride of Rollant;
Marvel it is, God stays so tolerant.
1775 Noples he took, not waiting your command;
Thence issued forth the Sarrazins, a band
With vassalage had fought against Rollant;
1777A He slew them first, with Durendal his brand,
Then washed their blood with water from the
      land;
So what he'd done might not be seen of man.
1780 He for a hare goes all day, horn in hand;
Before his peers in foolish jest he brags.

58

No race neath heav'n in field him dare attack.
So canter on ! Nay, wherefore hold we back ?
Terra Major is far away, our land."

CXXXV

1785 The count Rollanz, though blood his mouth doth
        stain,
And burst are both the temples of his brain,
His olifant he sounds with grief and pain ;
Charlès hath heard, listen the Franks again.
" That horn," the King says, " hath a mighty
        strain ! "
1790 Answers Duke Niemes : " A baron blows with
        pain !
Battle is there, indeed I see it plain,
He is betrayed, by one that still doth feign.
Equip you, sir, cry out your old refrain,
That noble band, go succour them amain !
1795 Enough you've heard how Rollant doth com-
        plain."

CXXXVI

That Emperour hath bid them sound their horns.
The Franks dismount, and dress themselves for
        war,
Put hauberks on, helmets and golden swords ;
Fine shields they have, and spears of length and
        force
1800 Scarlat and blue and white their ensigns float.
His charger mounts each baron of the host ;
They spur with haste as through the pass they go.
Nor was there one but thus to 's neighbour spoke :
" Now, ere he die, may we see Rollant, so
1805 Ranged by his side we'll give some goodly blows."
But what avail ? They've stayed too long below.

CXXXVII

That even-tide is light as was the day ;
Their armour shines beneath the sun's clear ray,

Hauberks and helms throw off a dazzling flame,
1810 And blazoned shields, flowered in bright array,
Also their spears, with golden ensigns gay.
That Emperour, he canters on with rage,
And all the Franks with wonder and dismay ;
There is not one can bitter tears restrain,
1815 And for Rollant they're very sore afraid.
The King has bid them seize that county Guene,
And charged with him the scullions of his train ;
The master-cook he's called, Besgun by name :
" Guard me him well, his felony is plain,
1820 Who in my house vile treachery has made."
He holds him, and a hundred others takes
From the kitchen, both good and evil knaves ;
Then Guenè's beard and both his cheeks they
        shaved,
And four blows each with their closed fists they
        gave,
1825 They trounced him well with cudgels and with
        staves,
And on his neck they clasped an iron chain ;
So like a bear enchained they held him safe,
On a pack-mule they set him in his shame :
Kept him till Charles should call for him again.

CXXXVIII

1830 High were the peaks and shadowy and grand,
The valleys deep, the rivers swiftly ran.
Trumpets they blew in rear and in the van,
Till all again answered that olifant.
That Emperour canters with fury mad,
1835 And all the Franks dismay and wonder have ;
There is not one but weeps and waxes sad
And all pray God that He will guard Rollant
Till in the field together they may stand ;
There by his side they'll strike as well they can.
1840 But what avail ? No good there is in that ;
They're not in time ; too long have they held
        back.

CXXXIX

In his great rage on canters Charlemagne ;
Over his sark his beard is flowing plain.
Barons of France, in haste they spur and strain ;
1845 There is not one that can his wrath contain
That they are not with Rollant the Captain,
Whereas he fights the Sarrazins of Spain.
If he be struck, will not one soul remain.
—God ! Sixty men are all now in his train !
1850 Never a king had better Capitans.

CXL

Rollant regards the barren mountain-sides ;
Dead men of France, he sees so many lie,
And weeps for them as fits a gentle knight :
" Lords and barons, may God to you be kind !
1855 And all your souls redeem for Paradise !
And let you there mid holy flowers lie !
Better vassals than you saw never I.
Ever you've served me, and so long a time,
By you Carlon hath conquered kingdoms wide ;
1860 That Emperour reared you for evil plight !
Douce land of France, o very precious clime,
Laid desolate by such a sour exile !
Barons of France, for me I've seen you die,
And no support, no warrant could I find ;
1865 God be your aid, Who never yet hath lied !
I must not fail now, brother, by your side ;
Save I be slain, for sorrow shall I die.
Sir companion, let us again go strike ! "

CXLI

The count Rollanz, back to the field then hieing
1870 Holds Durendal, and like a vassal striking
Faldrun of Pui has through the middle slicèd,
With twenty-four of all they rated highest ;
Was never man, for vengeance shewed such
    liking.
Even as a stag before the hounds goes flying,

1875   Before Rollanz the pagans scatter, frightened.
Says the Archbishop : " You deal now very
     wisely !
Such valour should he shew that is bred knightly,
And beareth arms, and a good charger rideth ;
In battle should be strong and proud and
     sprightly ;
1880   Or otherwise he is not worth a shilling,
Should be a monk in one of those old minsters,
Where, day by day, he'ld pray for us poor
     sinners."
Answers Rollant : " Strike on ; no quarter give
     them ! "
Upon these words Franks are again beginning ;
1885   Very great loss they suffer then, the Christians.

CXLII

The man who knows, for him there's no prison,
In such a fight with keen defence lays on ;
Wherefore the Franks are fiercer than lions.
Marsile you'd seen go as a brave baron,
1890   Sitting his horse, the which he calls Gaignon ;
He spurs it well, going to strike Bevon,
That was the lord of Beaune and of Dijon,
His shield he breaks, his hauberk has undone,
So flings him dead, without condition ;
1895   Next he hath slain Yvoerie and Ivon,
Also with them Gerard of Russillon.
The count Rollanz, being not far him from,
To th'pagan says : " Confound thee our Lord
     God !
So wrongfully you've slain my companions,
1900   A blow you'll take, ere we apart be gone,
And of my sword the name I'll bid you con."
He goes to strike him, as a brave baron,
And his right hand the count clean slices off ;
Then takes the head of Jursaleu the blond ;
1905   That was the son of king Marsilion.
Pagans cry out : " Assist us now, Mahom !
God of our race, avenge us on Carlon !

Into this land he's sent us such felons
That will not leave the fight before they drop."
1910 Says each to each : " Nay let us fly ! " Upon
That word, they're fled, an hundred thousand
        gone ;
Call them who may, they'll never more come on.

CXLIII

But what avail ? Though fled be Marsilies,
He's left behind his uncle, the alcaliph
1915 Who holds Alferne, Kartagene, Garmalie,
And Ethiope, a cursèd land indeed ;
The blackamoors from there are in his keep,
Broad in the nose they are and flat in the ear,
Fifty thousand and more in company.
1920 These canter forth with arrogance and heat,
Then they cry out the pagans' rallying-cheer ;
And Rollant says : " Martyrdom we'll receive ;
Not long to live, I know it well, have we ;
Felon he's named that sells his body cheap !
1925 Strike on, my lords, with burnished swords and
        keen ;
Contest each inch your life and death between,
That ne'er by us Douce France in shame be
        steeped.
When Charles my lord shall come into this field,
Such discipline of Sarrazins he'll see,
1930 For one of ours he'll find them dead fifteen ;
He will not fail, but bless us all in peace."

CXLIV

When Rollant sees those misbegotten men,
Who are more black than ink is on the pen
With no part white, only their teeth except,
1935 Then says that count : " I know now very well
That here to die we're bound, as I can tell.
Strike on, the Franks ! For so I recommend."
Says Oliver : " Who holds back, is condemned!"
Upon those words, the Franks to strike again.

CXLV

1940 Franks are but few ; which, when the pagans
   know,
  Among themselves comfort and pride they shew;
  Says each to each : " Wrong was that Emperor."
  Their alcaliph upon a sorrel rode,
  And pricked it well with both his spurs of gold ;
1945 Struck Oliver, behind, on the back-bone,
  His hauberk white into his body broke,
  Clean through his breast the thrusting spear he
   drove ;
  After he said : " You've borne a mighty blow.
  Charlès the great should not have left you so ;
1950 He's done us wrong, small thanks to him we owe ;
  I've well avenged all ours on you alone."

CXLVI

  Oliver feels that he to die is bound,
  Holds Halteclere, whose steel is rough and brown,
  Strikes the alcaliph on his helm's golden mount ;
1955 Flowers and stones fall clattering to the ground,
  Slices his head, to th'small teeth in his mouth ;
  So brandishes his blade and flings him down ;
  After he says : " Pagan, accurst be thou !
  Thou'lt never say that Charles forsakes me now ;
1960 Nor to thy wife, nor any dame thou'st found,
  Thou'lt never boast, in lands where thou wast
   crowned,
  One pennyworth from me thou'st taken out,
  Nor damage wrought on me nor any around."
  After, for aid, " Rollant ! " he cries aloud.

CXLVII

1965 Oliver feels that death is drawing nigh ;
  To avenge himself he hath no longer time ;
  Through the great press most gallantly he strikes,
  He breaks their spears, their buckled shields doth
   slice,

Their feet, their fists, their shoulders and their
    sides,
1970 Dismembers them : whoso had seen that sight,
Dead in the field one on another piled,
Remember well a vassal brave he might.
Charlè's ensign he'll not forget it quite ;
Aloud and clear " Monjoie " again he cries.
1975 To call Rollanz, his friend and peer, he tries :
" My companion, come hither to my side.
With bitter grief we must us now divide."

CXLVIII

Then Rollant looked upon Olivier's face ;
Which was all wan and colourless and pale,
1980 While the clear blood, out of his body sprayed,
Upon the ground gushed forth and ran away.
" God ! " said that count, " What shall I do or
    say ?
My companion, gallant for such ill fate !
Ne'er shall man be, against thee could prevail.
1985 Ah ! France the Douce, henceforth art thou
    made waste
Of vassals brave, confounded and disgraced !
Our Emperour shall suffer damage great."
And with these words upon his horse he faints.

CXLIX

You'd seen Rollant aswoon there in his seat,
1990 And Oliver, who unto death doth bleed,
So much he's bled, his eyes are dim and weak ;
Nor clear enough his vision, far or near,
To recognise whatever man he sees ;
His companion, when each the other meets,
1995 Above the helm jewelled with gold he beats,
Slicing it down from there to the nose-piece,
But not his head ; he's touched not brow nor
    cheek.
At such a blow Rollant regards him keen,
And asks of him, in gentle tones and sweet :

2000 " To do this thing, my comrade, did you mean ?
This is Rollanz, who ever held you dear ;
And no mistrust was ever us between."
Says Oliver : " Now can I hear you speak ;
I see you not : may the Lord God you keep !
2005 I struck you now : and for your pardon plead."
Answers Rollanz : " I am not hurt, indeed ;
I pardon you, before God's Throne and here."
Upon these words, each to the other leans ;
And in such love you had their parting seen.

CL

2010 Oliver feels death's anguish on him now ;
And in his head his two eyes swimming round ;
Nothing he sees ; he hears not any sound ;
Dismounting then, he kneels upon the ground,
Proclaims his sins both firmly and aloud,
2015 Clasps his two hands, heavenwards holds them
out,
Prays God himself in Paradise to allow ;
Blessings on Charles, and on Douce France he
vows,
And his comrade, Rollanz, to whom he's bound.
Then his heart fails ; his helmet nods and bows;
2020 Upon the earth he lays his whole length out :
And he is dead, may stay no more, that count.
Rollanz the brave mourns him with grief pro-
found ;
Nowhere on earth so sad a man you'd found.

CLI

So Rollant's friend is dead ; whom when he sees
2025 Face to the ground, and biting it with's teeth,
Begins to mourn in language very sweet :
" Unlucky, friend, your courage was indeed !
Together we have spent such days and years ;
No harmful thing twixt thee and me has been.
2030 Now thou art dead, and all my life a grief."
And with these words again he swoons, that chief,

66

Upon his horse, which he calls Veillantif;
Stirrups of gold support him underneath;
He cannot fall, whichever way he lean.

CLII

2035 Soon as Rollant his senses won and knew,
Recovering and turning from that swoon.
Bitter great loss appeared there in his view:
Dead are the Franks; he'd all of them to lose,
Save the Archbishop, and save Gualter del Hum;
2040 He is come down out of the mountains, who
Gainst Spanish men made there a great ado;
Dead are his men, for those the pagans slew;
Will he or nill, along the vales he flew,
And called Rollant, to bring him succour soon:
2045 "Ah! Gentle count, brave soldier, where are
    you?
For by thy side no fear I ever knew.
Gualter it is, who conquered Maëlgut,
And nephew was to hoary old Droün;
My vassalage thou ever thoughtest good.
2050 Broken my spear, and split my shield in two;
Gone is the mail that on my hauberk grew;
This body of mine eight lances have gone through;
I'm dying. Yet full price for life I took."
Rollant has heard these words and understood,
2055 Has spurred his horse, and on towards him drew.

CLIII

Grief gives Rollanz intolerance and pride;
Through the great press he goes again to strike;
To slay a score of Spaniards he contrives,
Gualter has six, the Archbishop other five.
2060 The pagans say: "Men, these, of felon kind!
Lordings, take care they go not hence alive!
Felon he's named that does not break their line,
Recreant, who lets them any safety find!"
And so once more begin the hue and cry,
2065 From every part they come to break the line.

67

CLIV

Count Rollant is a noble and brave soldier,
Gualter del Hum's a right good chevalier,
That Archbishop hath shewn good prowess there;
None of them falls behind the other pair ;
2070 Through the great press, pagans they strike again.
Come on afoot a thousand Sarrazens,
And on horseback some forty thousand men.
But well I know, to approach they never dare ;
Lances and spears they poise to hurl at them,
2075 Arrows, barbs, darts and javelins in the air.
With the first flight they've slain our Gualtïer ;
Turpin of Reims has all his shield broken,
And cracked his helm ; he's wounded in the
        head,
From his hauberk the woven mail they tear,
2080 In his body four spear-wounds doth he bear ;
Beneath him too his charger's fallen dead.
Great grief it was, when that Archbishop fell.

CLV

Turpin of Reims hath felt himself undone,
Since that four spears have through his body
        come ;
2085 Nimble and bold upon his feet he jumps ;
Looks for Rollant, and then towards him runs,
Saying this word : " I am not overcome.
While life remains, no good vassal gives up."
He's drawn Almace, whose steel was brown and
        rough,
2090 Through the great press a thousand blows he's
        struck :
As Charlès said, quarter he gave to none ;
He found him there, four hundred else among,
Wounded the most, speared through the middle
        some,
Also there were from whom the heads he'd cut :
2095 So tells the tale, he that was there says thus,
The brave Saint Giles, whom God made mar-
        vellous,

68

Who charters wrote for th' Minster at Loüm ;
Nothing he's heard that does not know this much.

CLVI

The count Rollanz has nobly fought and well,
2100 But he is hot, and all his body sweats ;
Great pain he has, and trouble in his head,
His temples burst when he the horn sounded ;
But he would know if Charles will come to them,
Takes the olifant, and feebly sounds again.
2105 That Emperour stood still and listened then :
" My lords," said he, " Right evilly we fare !
This day Rollanz, my nephew shall be dead :
I hear his horn, with scarcely any breath.
Nimbly canter, whoever would be there !
2110 Your trumpets sound, as many as ye bear ! "
Sixty thousand so loud together blare,
The mountains ring, the valleys answer them.
The pagans hear, they think it not a jest ;
Says each to each : " Carlum doth us beset."

CLVII

2115 The pagans say : " That Emperour's at hand,
We hear their sound, the trumpets of the Franks;
If Charles come, great loss we then shall stand,
And wars renewed, unless we slay Rollant ;
All Spain we'll lose, our own clear father-land."
2120 Four hundred men of them in helmets stand ;
The best of them that might be in their ranks
Make on Rollanz a grim and fierce attack ;
Gainst these the count had well enough in hand.

CLVIII

The count Rollanz, when their approach he sees
2125 Is grown so bold and manifest and fierce
So long as he's alive he will not yield.
He sits his horse, which men call Veillantif,
Pricking him well with golden spurs beneath,

Through the great press he goes, their line to
    meet,
2130   And by his side is the Archbishop Turpin.
"Now, friend, begone!" say pagans, each to
    each;
"These Frankish men, their horns we plainly
    hear;
Charle is at hand, that King in Majesty."

CLIX

The count Rollanz has never loved cowards,
2135   Nor arrogant, nor men of evil heart,
Nor chevalier that was not good vassal.
That Archbishop, Turpins, he calls apart:
"Sir, you're afoot, and I my charger have;
For love of you, here will I take my stand,
2140   Together we'll endure things good and bad;
I'll leave you not, for no incarnate man:
We'll give again these pagans their attack;
The better blows are those from Durendal."
Says the Archbishop: "Shame on him that holds
    back!
2145   Charle is at hand, full vengeance he'll exact."

CLX

The pagans say: "Unlucky were we born!
An evil day for us did this day dawn!
For we have lost our peers and all our lords.
Charles his great host once more upon us draws,
2150   Of Frankish men we plainly hear the horns,
"Monjoie" they cry, and great is their uproar.
The count Rollant is of such pride and force
He'll never yield to man of woman born;
Let's aim at him, then leave him on the spot!"
2155   And aim they did: with arrows long and short,
Lances and spears and feathered javelots;
Count Rollant's shield they've broken through
    and bored,
The woven mail have from his hauberk torn,

But not himself, they've never touched his corse ;
2160 Veillantif is in thirty places gored,
Beneath the count he's fallen dead, that horse.
Pagans are fled, and leave him on the spot ;
The count Rollant stands on his feet once more.

CLXI

Pagans are fled, enangered and enraged,
2165 Home into Spain with speed they make their
way ;
The count Rollanz, he has not given chase,
For Veillantif, his charger, they have slain ;
Will he or nill, on foot he must remain.
To the Archbishop, Turpins, he goes with aid ;
2170 He's from his head the golden helm unlaced,
Taken from him his white hauberk away,
And cut the gown in strips, was round his waist ;
On his great wounds the pieces of it placed,
Then to his heart has caught him and embraced;
2175 On the green grass he has him softly laid,
Most sweetly then to him has Rollant prayed :
" Ah ! Gentle sir, give me your leave, I say ;
Our companions, whom we so dear appraised,
Are now all dead ; we cannot let them stay ;
2180 I will go seek and bring them to this place,
Arrange them here in ranks, before your face."
Said the Archbishop : " Go, and return again.
This field is yours and mine now ; God be
praised ! "

CLXII

So Rollanz turns ; through the field, all alone,
2185 Searching the vales and mountains, he is gone ;
He finds Gerin, Gerers his companion,
Also he finds Berenger and Otton,
There too he finds Anséis and Sanson,
And finds Gerard the old, of Rossillon ;
2190 By one and one he's taken those barons,
To the Archbishop with each of them he comes,

71

Before his knees arranges every one.
That Archbishop, he cannot help but sob,
He lifts his hand, gives benediction ;
2195 After he's said : " Unlucky, Lords, your lot !
But all your souls He'll lay, our Glorious God,
In Paradise, His holy flowers upon !
For my own death such anguish now I've got ;
I shall not see him, our rich Emperor."

CLXIII

2200 So Rollant turns, goes through the field in quest ;
His companion Olivier finds at length ;
He has embraced him close against his breast,
To the Archbishop returns as he can best ;
Upon a shield he's laid him, by the rest ;
2205 And the Archbishop has them absolved and blest:
Whereon his grief and pity grow afresh.
Then says Rollanz : " Fair comrade Olivier,
You were the son of the good count Reinier,
Who held the march by th' Vale of Runier ;
2210 To shatter spears, through buckled shields to
        bear,
And from hauberks the mail to break and tear,
Proof men to lead, and prudent counsel share,
Gluttons in field to frighten and conquer,
No land has known a better chevalier."

CLXIV

2215 The count Rollanz, when dead he saw his peers,
And Oliver, he held so very dear,
Grew tender, and began to shed a tear ;
Out of his face the colour disappeared ;
No longer could he stand, for so much grief,
2220 Will he or nill, he swooned upon the field.
Said the Archbishop : " Unlucky lord, indeed !"

CLXV

When the Archbishop beheld him swoon, Rollant,
Never before such bitter grief he'd had ;

Stretching his hand, he took that olifant.
2225 Through Rencesvals a little river ran ;
He would go there, fetch water for Rollant.
Went step by step, to stumble soon began,
So feeble he is, no further fare he can,
For too much blood he's lost, and no strength
has ;
2230 Ere he has crossed an acre of the land,
His heart grows faint, he falls down forwards
and
Death comes to him with very cruel pangs.

CLXVI

The count Rollanz wakes from his swoon once
more,
Climbs to his feet ; his pains are very sore ;
2235 Looks down the vale, looks to the hills above ;
On the green grass, beyond his companions,
He sees him lie, that noble old baron ;
'Tis the Archbishop, whom in His name wrought
God ;
There he proclaims his sins, and looks above ;
2240 Joins his two hands, to Heaven holds them forth,
And Paradise prays God to him to accord.
Dead is Turpin, the warrior of Charlon.
In battles great and very rare sermons
Against pagans ever a champion.
2245 God grant him now His Benediction !

CLXVII

The count Rollant sees the Archbishop lie dead,
Sees the bowels out of his body shed,
And sees the brains that surge from his forehead;
Between his two arm-pits, upon his breast,
2250 Crossways he folds those hands so white and fair.
Then mourns aloud, as was the custom there :
" Thee, gentle sir, chevalier nobly bred,
To th' Glorious Celestial I commend ;
Ne'er shall man be, that will Him serve so well ;

73

2255   Since the Apostles was never such prophet,
To hold the laws and draw the hearts of men.
Now may your soul no pain nor sorrow ken,
Finding the gates of Paradise open ! "

CLXVIII

Then Rollanz feels that death to him draws near,
2260   For all his brain is issued from his ears ;
He prays to God that He will call the peers,
Bids Gabriel, the angel, t' himself appear.
Takes the olifant, that no reproach shall hear,
And Durendal in the other hand he wields ;
2265   Further than might a cross-bow's arrow speed
Goes towards Spain into a fallow-field ;
Climbs on a cliff ; where, under two fair trees,
Four terraces, of marble wrought, he sees.
There he falls down, and lies upon the green ;
2270   He swoons again, for death is very near.

CLXIX

High are the peaks, the trees are very high.
Four terraces of polished marble shine ;
On the green grass count Rollant swoons thereby.
A Sarrazin him all the time espies,
2275   Who feigning death among the others hides ;
Blood hath his face and all his body dyed ;
He gets afoot, running towards him hies ;
Fair was he, strong and of a courage high ;
A mortal hate he's kindled in his pride.
2280   He's seized Rollant, and the arms, were at his
side,
" Charlè's nephew," he's said, " here conquered
lies.
To Araby I'll bear this sword as prize."
As he drew it, something the count descried.

CLXX

So Rollant felt his sword was taken forth,
2285   Opened his eyes, and this word to him spoke :

74

"Thou'rt never one of ours, full well I know."
Took the olifant, that he would not let go,
Struck him on th' helm, that jewelled was with
    gold,
And broke its steel, his skull and all his bones,
2290   Out of his head both the two eyes he drove ;
Dead at his feet he has the pagan thrown :
After he's said : " Culvert, thou wert too bold,
Or right or wrong, of my sword seizing hold !
They'll dub thee fool, to whom the tale is told.
2295   But my great one, my olifant I broke ;
Fallen from it the crystal and the gold."

CLXXI

Then Rollanz feels that he has lost his sight,
Climbs to his feet, uses what strength he might ;
In all his face the colour is grown white.
2300   In front of him a great brown boulder lies ;
Whereon ten blows with grief and rage he strikes;
The steel cries out, but does not break outright ;
And the count says : " Saint Mary, be my guide !
Good Durendal, unlucky is your plight !
2305   I've need of you no more ; spent is my pride !
We in the field have won so many fights,
Combating through so many regions wide
That Charlès holds, whose beard is hoary white !
Be you not his that turns from any in flight !
2310   A good vassal has held you this long time ;
Never shall France the Free behold his like."

CLXXII

Rollant hath struck the sardonyx terrace ;
The steel cries out, but broken is no ways.
So when he sees he never can it break,
2315   Within himself begins he to complain :
" Ah ! Durendal, white art thou, clear of stain !
Beneath the sun reflecting back his rays !
In Moriane was Charlès, in the vale,
When from heaven God by His angel bade

75

2320 Him give thee to a count and capitain ;
Girt thee on me that noble King and great.
I won for him with thee Anjou, Bretaigne,
And won for him with thee Peitou, the Maine,
And Normandy the free for him I gained,
2325 Also with thee Provence and Equitaigne,
And Lumbardie and all the whole Romaigne,
I won Baivere, all Flanders in the plain,
Also Burguigne and all the whole Puillane,
Costentinnople, that homage to him pays ;
2330 In Saisonie all is as he ordains ;
With thee I won him Scotland, Ireland, Wales,
England also, where he his chamber makes ;
Won I with thee so many countries strange
That Charlès holds, whose beard is white with
age !
2335 For this sword's sake sorrow upon me weighs,
Rather I'ld die, than it mid pagans stay.
Lord God Father, never let France be shamed !"

CLXXIII

Rollant his stroke on a dark stone repeats,
And more of it breaks off than I can speak.
2340 The sword cries out, yet breaks not in the least,
Back from the blow into the air it leaps.
Destroy it can he not ; which when he sees,
Within himself he makes a plaint most sweet :
" Ah ! Durendal, most holy, fair indeed !
2345 Relics enough thy golden hilt conceals :
Saint Peter's Tooth, the Blood of Saint Basile,
Some of the Hairs of my Lord, Saint Denise,
Some of the Robe, was worn by Saint Mary.
It is not right that pagans should thee seize,
2350 For Christian men thy use shall ever be.
Nor any man's that worketh cowardice !
Many broad lands with thee have I retrieved
Which Charles holds, who hath the great white
beard ;
Wherefore that King so proud and rich is he."

CLXXIV

2355 But Rollant felt that death had made a way
Down from his head till on his heart it lay ;
Beneath a pine running in haste he came,
On the green grass he lay there on his face ;
His olifant and sword beneath him placed,
2360 Turning his head towards the pagan race,
Now this he did, in truth, that Charles might say
(As he desired) and all the Franks his race ;—
' Ah, gentle count ; conquering he was slain !'—
He owned his faults often and every way,
2365 And for his sins his glove to God upraised.

CLXXV

But Rollant feels he's no more time to seek ;
Looking to Spain, he lies on a sheer peak,
And with one hand upon his breast he beats :
" *Mea Culpa !* God, by Thy Virtues clean
2370 Me from my sins, the mortal and the mean,
Which from the hour that I was born have been
Until this day, when life is ended here ! "
Holds out his glove towards God, as he speaks ;
Angels descend from heaven on that scene.

CLXXVI

2375 The count Rollanz, beneath a pine he sits ;
Turning his eyes towards Spain, he begins
Remembering so many divers things :
So many lands where he went conquering,
And France the Douce, the heroes of his kin,
2380 And Charlemagne, his lord who nourished him.
Nor can he help but weep and sigh at this.
But his own self, he's not forgotten him,
He owns his faults, and God's forgiveness bids :
" Very Father, in Whom no falsehood is,
2385 Saint Lazaron from death Thou didst remit,
And Daniel save from the lions' pit ;
My soul in me preserve from all perils
And from the sins I did in life commit ! "

His right-hand glove, to God he offers it ;
2390 Saint Gabriel from 's hand hath taken it.
Over his arm his head bows down and slips,
He joins his hands : and so is life finish'd.
God sent him down His angel cherubin,
And Saint Michael, we worship in peril ;
2395 And by their side Saint Gabriel alit ;
So the count's soul they bare to Paradis.

CLXXVII

Rollant is dead ; his soul to heav'n God bare.
That Emperour to Rencesvals doth fare.
There was no path nor passage anywhere
2400 Nor of waste ground no ell nor foot to spare
Without a Frank or pagan lying there.
Charles cries aloud : " Where are you, nephew
        fair ?
Where's the Archbishop and that count Oliviers?
Where is Gerins and his comrade Gerers ?
2405 Otès the Duke, and the count Berengiers
And Ivorie, and Ive, so dear they were ?
What is become of Gascon Engelier,
Sansun the Duke and Anséis the fierce ?
Where's old Gerard of Russillun ; oh, where
2410 The dozen peers I left behind me there ? "
But what avail, since none can answer bear ?
" God ! " says the King, " Now well may I
        despair,
I was not here the first assault to share ! "
Seeming enraged, his beard the King doth tear.
2415 Weep from their eyes barons and chevaliers,
A thousand score, they swoon upon the earth ;
Duke Neimes for them was ·moved with pity
        rare.

CLXXVIII

No chevalier nor baron is there, who
Pitifully weeps not for grief and dule ;
2420 They mourn their sons, their brothers, their
        nephews,

78

And their liege lords, and trusty friends and true;
Upon the ground a many of them swoon.
Thereon Duke Neimes doth act with wisdom
    proof,
First before all he's said to the Emperour :
2425   " See beforehand, a league from us or two,
From the highways dust rising in our view ;
Pagans are there, and many of them, too.
Canter therefore ! Vengeance upon them do ! "
" Ah, God ! " says Charles, " so far are they re-
    moved !
2430   Do right by me, my honour still renew !
They've torn from me the flower of France the
    Douce."
The King commands Gebuin and Otun,
Tedbalt of Reims, also the count Milun :
" Guard me this field, these hills and valleys too,
2435   Let the dead lie, all as they are, unmoved,
Let not approach lion, nor any brute,
Let not approach esquire, nor any groom ;
For I forbid that any come thereto,
Until God will that we return anew."
2440   These answer him sweetly, their love to prove :
" Right Emperour, dear Sire, so will we do."
A thousand knights they keep in retinue.

CLXXIX

That Emperour bids trumpets sound again,
Then canters forth with his great host so brave.
2445   Of Spanish men, whose backs are turned their
    way,
Franks one and all continue in their chase.
When the King sees the light at even fade,
On the green grass dismounting as he may,
He kneels aground, to God the Lord doth pray
2450   That the sun's course He will for him delay,
Put off the night, and still prolong the day.
An angel then, with him should reason make,
Nimbly enough appeared to him and spake :

79

"Charles, canter on ! Light needst not thou
  await.
2455 The flower of France, as God knows well, is
  slain ;
Thou canst be avenged upon that crimeful race."
Upon that word mounts the Emperour again.

CLXXX

For Charlemagne a great marvel God planned :
Making the sun still in his course to stand.
2460 So pagans fled, and chased them well the Franks
Through the Valley of Shadows, close in hand ;
Towards Sarraguce by force they chased them
  back,
And as they went with killing blows attacked :
Barred their highways and every path they had.
2465 The River Sebre before them reared its bank,
'Twas very deep, marvellous current ran ;
No barge thereon nor dromond nor caland.
A god of theirs invoked they, Tervagant.
And then leaped in, but there no warrant had.
2470 The armèd men more weighty were for that,
Many of them down to the bottom sank,
Downstream the rest floated as they might hap ;
So much water the luckiest of them drank,
That all were drowned, with marvellous keen
  pangs.
2475 "An evil day," cry Franks, "ye saw Rollant !"

CLXXXI

When Charlès sees that pagans all are dead,
Some of them slain, the greater part drownèd ;
(Whereby great spoils his chevaliers collect)
That gentle King upon his feet descends,
2480 Kneels on the ground, his thanks to God pre-
  sents.
When he once more rises, the sun is set.
Says the Emperour : "Time is to pitch our tents ;

80

To Rencesvals too late to go again.
Our horses are worn out and founderèd :
2485 Unsaddle them, take bridles from their heads,
And through these meads let them refreshment
get."
Answer the Franks : " Sire, you have spoken
well."

CLXXXII

That Emperour hath chosen his bivouac ;
The Franks dismount in those deserted tracts,
2490 Their saddles take from off their horses' backs,
Bridles of gold from off their heads unstrap,
Let them go free ; there is enough fresh grass —
No service can they render them, save that.
Who is most tired sleeps on the ground stretched
flat.
2495 Upon this night no sentinels keep watch.

CLXXXIII

That Emperour is lying in a mead ;
By 's head, so brave, he's placed his mighty spear ;
On such a night unarmed he will not be.
He's donned his white hauberk, with broidery,
2500 Has laced his helm, jewelled with golden beads,
Girt on Joiuse, there never was its peer,
Whereon each day thirty fresh hues appear.
All of us know that lance, and well may speak
Whereby Our Lord was wounded on the Tree :
2505 Charles, by God's grace, possessed its point of
steel !
His golden hilt he enshrined it underneath.
By that honour and by that sanctity
The name Joiuse was for that sword decreed.
Barons of France may not forgetful be
2510 Whence comes the ensign " Monjoie," they cry
at need ;
Wherefore no race against them can succeed.

81

CLXXXIV

Clear was the night, the moon shone radiant.
Charles laid him down, but sorrow for Rollant
And Oliver, most heavy on him he had,
2515   For 's dozen peers, for all the Frankish band
He had left dead in bloody Rencesvals ;
He could not help, but wept and waxèd mad,
And prayed to God to be their souls' Warrant.
Weary that King, for grief he's very sad ;
2520   He falls on sleep, he can no more withstand.
Through all those meads they slumber then, the
     Franks ;
Is not a horse can any longer stand,
Who would eat grass, he takes it lying flat.
He has learned much, can understand their pangs.

CLXXXV

2525   Charles, like a man worn out with labour, slept.
Saint Gabriel the Lord to him hath sent,
Whom as a guard o'er the Emperour He set ;
Stood all night long that angel by his head.
In a vision announced he to him then
2530   A battle, should be fought against him yet,
Significance of griefs demonstrated.
Charlès looked up towards the sky, and there
Thunders and winds and blowing gales beheld,
And hurricanes and marvellous tempests ;
2535   Lightnings and flames he saw in readiness,
That speedily on all his people fell ;
Apple and ash, their spear-shafts all burnèd,
Also their shields, e'en the golden bosses,
Crumbled the shafts of their trenchant lances,
2540   Crushed their hauberks and all their steel helmets.
His chevaliers he saw in great distress.
Bears and leopards would feed upon them next ;
Adversaries, dragons, wyverns, serpents,
Griffins were there, thirty thousand, no less,
2545   Nor was there one but on some Frank it set.
And the Franks cried : " Ah ! Charlemagne,
     give help ! "

Wherefore the King much grief and pity felt,
He'ld go to them but was in duress kept :
Out of a wood came a great lion then,
2550 'Twas very proud and fierce and terrible ;
His body dear sought out, and on him leapt,
Each in his arms, wrestling, the other held ;
But he knew not which conquered, nor which fell.
That Emperour woke not at all, but slept.

CLXXXVI

2555 And, after that, another vision came :
Himseemed in France, at Aix, on a terrace,
And that he held a bruin by two chains ;
Out of Ardenne saw thirty bears that came,
And each of them words, as a man might, spake :
2560 Said to him : " Sire, give him to us again !
It is not right that he with you remain,
He's of our kin, and we must lend him aid."
A harrier fair ran out of his palace,
Among them all the greatest bear assailed
2565 On the green grass, beyond his friends some way.
There saw the King marvellous give and take ;
But he knew not which fell, nor which o'ercame.
The angel of God so much to him made plain.
Charlès slept on till the clear dawn of day.

CLXXXVII

2570 King Marsilies, fleeing to Sarraguce,
Dismounted there beneath an olive cool ;
His sword and sark and helm aside he put,
On the green grass lay down in shame and gloom;
For his right hand he'd lost, 'twas clean cut
     through ;
2575 Such blood he'd shed, in anguish keen he swooned.
Before his face his lady Bramimunde
Bewailed and cried, with very bitter rue ;
Twenty thousand and more around him stood,
All of them cursed Carlun and France the Douce.

*   *   *   *   *

2580 Then Apollin in's grotto they surround,
And threaten him, and ugly words pronounce :
"Such shame on us, vile god !, why bringest thou ?
This is our king ; wherefore dost him confound?
Who served thee oft, ill recompense hath found."
2585 Then they take off his sceptre and his crown,
With their hands hang him from a column down,
Among their feet trample him on the ground,
With great cudgels they batter him and trounce.
From Tervagant his carbuncle they impound,
2590 And Mahumet into a ditch fling out,
Where swine and dogs defile him and devour.

CLXXXVIII

Out of his swoon awakens Marsilies,
And has him borne his vaulted roof beneath ;
Many colours were painted there to see,
2595 And Bramimunde laments for him, the queen,
Tearing her hair ; caitiff herself she clepes ;
Also these words cries very loud and clear :
" Ah ! Sarraguce, henceforth forlorn thou'lt be
Of the fair king that had thee in his keep !
2600 All those our gods have wrought great felony,
Who in battle this morning failed at need.
That admiral will shew his cowardice,
Unless he fight against that race hardy,
Who are so fierce, for life they take no heed.
2605 That Emperour, with his blossoming beard,
Hath vassalage, and very high folly ;
Battle to fight, he will not ever flee.
Great grief it is, no man may slay him clean."

CLXXXIX

That Emperour, by his great Majesty,
2610 Full seven years in Spain now has he been,
And castles there, and many cities seized.
King Marsilies was therefore sore displeased ;
In the first year he sealed and sent his brief
To Baligant, into Babilonie :

84

2615 ('Twas the admiral, old in antiquity,
That clean outlived Omer and Virgilie,)
To Sarraguce, with succour bade him speed,
For, if he failed, Marsile his gods would leave,
All his idols he worshipped formerly ;
2620 He would receive blest Christianity
And reconciled to Charlemagne would be.
Long time that one came not, far off was he.
Through forty realms he did his tribes rally ;
His great dromonds, he made them all ready,
2625 Barges and skiffs and ships and galleries ;
Neath Alexandre, a haven next the sea,
In readiness he gat his whole navy.
That was in May, first summer of the year,
All of his hosts he launched upon the sea.

CXC

2630 Great are the hosts of that opposèd race ;
With speed they sail, they steer and navigate.
High on their yards, at their mast-heads they
place
Lanterns enough, and carbuncles so great
Thence, from above, such light they dissipate
2635 The sea's more 'clear at midnight than by day.
And when they come into the land of Spain
All that country lightens and shines again :
Of their coming Marsile has heard the tale.

CXCI

The pagan race would never rest, but come
2640 Out of the sea, where the sweet waters run ;
They leave Marbris, they leave behind Mar-
brus,
Upstream by Sebre doth all their navy turn.
Lanterns they have, and carbuncles enough,
That all night long and very clearly burn.
2645 Upon that day they come to Sarragus.

85

Clear is that day, and the sun radiant.
Out of his barge issues their admiral,
Espaneliz goes forth at his right hand,
Seventeen kings follow him in a band,
2650 Counts too, and dukes ; I cannot tell of that.
Where in a field, midway, a laurel stands,
On the green grass they spread a white silk mat,
Set a fald-stool there, made of olifant ;
Sits him thereon the pagan Baligant,
2655 And all the rest in rows about him stand.
The lord of them speaks before any man :
" Listen to me, free knights and valiant !
Charlès the King, the Emperour of the Franks,
Shall not eat bread, save whcn that I command.
2660 Throughout all Spain great war with me he's
had ;
I will go seek him now, into Douce France,
I will not cease, while I'm a living man,
Till be slain, or fall between my hands."
Upon his knee his right-hand glove he slaps.

CXCIII

2665 He is fast bound by all that he has said.
He will not fail, for all the gold neath heav'n,
But go to Aix, where Charlè's court is held :
His men applaud, for so they counsellèd.
After he called two of his chevaliers,
2670 One Clarifan, and the other Clarïen :
" You are the sons of king Maltraïen,
Freely was wont my messages to bear.
You I command to Sarraguce to fare.
Marsiliun on my part you shall tell
2675 Against the Franks I'm come to give him help,
Find I their host, great battle shall be there ;
Give him this glove, that's stitched with golden
thread,
On his right hand let it be worn and held ;
This little wand of fine gold take as well,

2680 Bid him come here, his homage to declare.
. To France I'll go, and war with Charles again ;
Save at my feet he kneel, and mercy beg,
Save all the laws of Christians he forget,
I'll take away the crown from off his head."
2685 Answer pagans : " Sire, you say very well."

CXCIV

Said Baligant : " But canter now, barons,
Take one the wand, and the other one the glove!"
These answer him : " Dear lord, it shall be
done."
Canter so far, to Sarraguce they come,
2690 Pass through ten gates, across four bridges run,
Through all the streets, wherein the burghers
crowd.
When they draw nigh the citadel above,
From the palace they hear a mighty sound ;
About that place are seen pagans enough,
2695 Who weep and cry, with grief are waxen wood,
And curse their gods, Tervagan and Mahum
And Apolin, from whom no help is come.
Says each to each : " Caitiffs ! What shall be
done ?
For upon us confusion vile is come,
2700 Now have we lost our king Marsiliun,
For yesterday his hand count Rollanz cut ;
We'll have no more Fair Jursaleu, his son ;
The whole of Spain henceforward is undone."
Both messengers on the terrace dismount.

CXCV

2705 Horses they leave under an olive tree,
Which by the reins two Sarrazins do lead ;
Those messengers have wrapped them in their
weeds,
To the palace they climb the topmost steep.
When they're come in, the vaulted roof beneath,
2710 Marsilium with courtesy they greet :

87

" May Mahumet, who all of us doth keep,
And Tervagant, and our lord Apoline
Preserve the king and guard from harm the
    queen ! "
Says Bramimunde : " Great foolishness I hear :
2715 Those gods of ours in cowardice are steeped ;
In Rencesvals they wrought an evil deed,
Our chevaliers they let be slain in heaps ;
My lord they failed in battle, in his need,
Never again will he his right hand see ;
2720 For that rich count, Rollanz, hath made him
    bleed.
All our whole Spain shall be for Charles to keep.
Miserable ! What shall become of me ?
Alas ! That I've no man to slay me clean ! "

CXCVI

Says Clarïen : " My lady, say not that !
2725 We're messengers from pagan Baligant ;
To Marsilies, he says, he'll be warrant,
So sends him here his glove, also this wand.
Vessels we have, are moored by Sebrè's bank,
Barges and skiffs and gallies four thousand,
2730 Dromonds are there—I cannot speak of that.
Our admiral is wealthy and puissant.
And Charlemagne he will go seek through France
And quittance give him, dead or recreant."
Says Bramimunde : " Unlucky journey, that !
2735 Far nearer here you'll light upon the Franks ;
For seven years he's stayed now in this land.
That Emperour is bold and combatant,
Rather he'ld die than from the field draw back ;
No king neath heav'n above a child he ranks.
2740 Charles hath no fear for any living man."

CXCVII

Says Marsilies the king : " Now let that be."
To th'messengers : " Sirs, pray you, speak to
    me.

I am held fast by death, as ye may see.
No son have I nor daughter to succeed ;
2745 That one I had, they slew him yester-eve.
Bid you my lord, he come to see me here.
That admiral, rights over Spain hath he,
My claim to him, if he will take't, I yield ;
But from the Franks he then must set her free.
2750 Gainst Charlemagne I'll shew him strategy.
Within a month from now he'll conquered be.
Of Sarraguce ye'll carry him the keys,
He'll go not hence, say, if he trusts in me."
They answer him : " Sir, 'tis the truth you speak."

CXCVIII

2755 Then says Marsile : " The Emperour, Charles
      the Great
Hath slain my men and all my land laid waste,
My cities are broken and violate ;
He lay this night upon the river Sebre ;
I've counted well, 'tis seven leagues away.
2760 Bid the admiral, leading his host this way,
Do battle here ; this word to him convey."
Gives them the keys of Sarraguce her gates ;
Both messengers their leave of him do take,
Upon that word bow down, and turn away.

CXCIX

2765 Both messengers did on their horses mount ;
From that city nimbly they issued out.
Then, sore afraid, their admiral they sought,
To whom the keys of Sarraguce they brought.
Says Baligant : " Speak now ; what have ye
      found ?
2770 Where's Marsilies, to come to me was bound ? "
Says Clariën : " To death he's stricken down.
That Emperour was in the pass but now ;
To France the Douce he would be homeward-
      bound,
Rereward he set, to save his great honour :

2775 His nephew there installed, Rollanz the count,
And Oliver ; the dozen peers around ;
A thousand score of Franks in armour found.
Marsile the king fought with them there, so
proud ;
He and Rollanz upon that field did joust.
2780 With Durendal he dealt him such a clout
From his body he cut the right hand down.
His son is dead, in whom his heart was bound,
And the barons that service to him vowed ;
Fleeing he came, he could no more hold out.
2785 That Emperour has chased him well enow.
The king implores, you'll hasten with succour,
Yields to you Spain, his kingdom and his crown."
And Baligant begins to think, and frowns ;
Such grief he has, doth nearly him confound.

CC

2790 " Sir admiral," said to him Clariens,
" In Rencesvals was yesterday battle.
Dead is Rollanz and that count Oliver,
The dozen peers whom Charle so cherishèd,
And of their Franks are twenty thousand dead.
2795 King Marsilie's of his right hand bereft,
And the Emperour chased him enow from thence.
Throughout this land no chevalier is left,
But he be slain, or drowned in Sebrè's bed.
By river side the Franks have pitched their tents,
2800 Into this land so near to us they've crept ;
But, if you will, grief shall go with them hence."
And Baligant looked on him proudly then,
In his courage grew joyous and content ;
From the fald-stool upon his feet he leapt,
2805 Then cried aloud : " Barons, too long ye've
slept ;
Forth from your ships issue, mount, canter well!
If he flee not, that Charlemagne the eld,
King Marsilies shall somehow be avenged ;
For his right hand I'll pay him back an head."

CCI

2810 Pagan Arabs out of their ships issue,
Then mount upon their horses and their mules,
And canter forth, (nay, what more might they
do ?)
Their admiral, by whom they all were ruled,
Called up to him Gemalfin, whom he knew :
2815 " I give command of all my hosts to you."
On a brown horse mounted, as he was used,
And in his train he took with him four dukes.
Cantered so far, he came to Sarraguce.
Dismounted on a floor of marble blue,
2820 Where four counts were, who by his stirrup
stood ;
Up by the steps, the palace came into ;
To meet him there came running Bramimunde,
Who said to him : " Accursèd from the womb,
That in such shame my sovran lord I lose ! "
2825 Fell at his feet ; that admiral her took.
In grief they came up into Marsile's room.

CCII

King Marsilies, when he sees Baligant,
Calls to him then two Spanish Sarazands :
" Take me by the arms, and so lift up my back."
2830 One of his gloves he takes in his left hand ;
Then says Marsile : " Sire, king and admiral,
Quittance I give you here of all my land,
With Sarraguce, and the honour thereto hangs.
Myself I've lost ; my army, every man."
2835 He answers him : " Therefore the more I'm
sad.
No long discourse together may we have ;
Full well I know, Charles waits not our attack,
I take the glove from you, in spite of that."
He turned away in tears, such grief he had.
2840 Down by the steps, out of the palace ran,
Mounted his horse, to's people gallopped back.
Cantered so far, he came before his band ;

From hour to hour then, as he went, he sang :
" Pagans, come on : already flee the Franks ! "

CCIII

2845 In morning time, when the dawn breaks at last,
Awakenèd is that Emperour Charles.
Saint Gabriel, who on God's part him guards,
Raises his hand, the Sign upon him marks.
Rises the King, his arms aside he's cast,
2850 The others then, through all the host, disarm.
After they mount, by virtue canter fast
Through those long ways, and through those
        roads so large ;
They go to see the marvellous damage
In Rencesvals, there where the battle was.

CCIV

2855 In Rencesvals is Charlès enterèd,
Begins to weep for those he finds there dead ;
Says to the Franks : " My lords, restrain your
        steps,
Since I myself alone should go ahead,
For my nephew, whom I would find again.
2860 At Aix I was, upon the feast Noel,
Vaunted them there my valiant chevaliers,
Of battles great and very hot contests ;
With reason thus I heard Rollant speak then :
He would not die in any foreign realm
2865 Ere he'd surpassed his peers and all his men.
To the foes' land he would have turned his head,
Conqueringly his gallant life he'ld end."
Further than one a little wand could send,
Before the rest he's on a peak mounted.

CCV

2870 When the Emperour went seeking his nephew,
He found the grass, and every flower that bloomed ;
Turned scarlat, with our barons' blood imbrued,

92

Pity he felt, he could but weep for rue.
Beneath two trees he climbed the hill and looked,
2875 And Rollant's strokes on three terraces knew,
On the green grass saw lying his nephew ;
'Tis nothing strange that Charlè's anger grew.
Dismounted then, and went—his heart was full,
In his two hands the count's body he took ;
2880 With anguish keen he fell on him and swooned.

CCVI

That Emperour is from his swoon revived.
Naimès the Duke, and the count Aceline,
Gefrei d'Anjou and his brother Tierry,
Take up the King, bear him beneath a pine.
2885 There on the ground he sees his nephew lie.
Most sweetly then begins he to repine :
" Rollant, my friend, may God to thee be
      kind !
Never beheld any man such a knight
So to engage and so to end a fight.
2890 Now my honour is turned into decline ! "
Charle swoons again, he cannot stand upright.

CCVII

Charlès the King returned out of his swoon.
Him in their hands four of his barons took,
He looked to the earth, saw lying his nephew ;
2895 All colourless his lusty body grew,
He turned his eyes, were very shadowful.
Charlès complained in amity and truth :
" Rollant, my friend, God lay thee mid the
      blooms
Of Paradise, among the glorious !
2900 Thou cam'st to Spain in evil tide, seigneur !
Day shall not dawn, for thee I've no dolour.
How perishes my strength and my valour !
None shall I have now to sustain my honour ;
I think I've not one friend neath heaven's roof,
2905 Kinsmen I have, but none of them's so proof."

He tore his locks, till both his hands were full.
Five score thousand Franks had such great
    dolour
There was not one but sorely wept for rue.

CCVIII

" Rollant, my friend, to France I will away ;
2910 When at Loüm, I'm in my hall again,
Strange men will come from many far domains,
Who'll ask me, where's that count, the Capitain ;
I'll say to them that he is dead in Spain.
In bitter grief henceforward shall I reign,
2915 Day shall not dawn, I weep not nor complain.

CCIX

" Rollant, my friend, fair youth that bar'st the
    bell,
When I arrive at Aix, in my Chapelle,
Men coming there will ask what news I tell ;
I'll say to them : ' Marvellous news and fell.
2920 My nephew's dead, who won for me such realms!'
Against me then the Saxon will rebel,
Hungar, Bulgar, and many hostile men,
Romain, Puillain, all those are in Palerne,
And in Affrike, and those in Califerne ;
2925 Afresh then will my pain and suffrance swell.
For who will lead my armies with such strength,
When he is slain, that all our days us led ?
Ah ! France the Douce, now art thou deserted !
Such grief I have that I would fain be dead."
2930 All his white beard he hath begun to rend,
Tore with both hands the hair out of his head.
Five score thousand Franks swooned on the earth
    and fell.

CCX

" Rollant, my friend, God shew thee His mercy !
In Paradise repose the soul of thee !
2935 Who hath thee slain, exile for France decreed.
I'ld live no more, so bitter is my grief

94

For my household, who have been slain for me.
God grant me this, the Son of Saint Mary,
Ere I am come to th' master-pass of Size,
2940 From my body my soul at length go free !
Among their souls let mine in glory be,
And let my flesh upon their flesh be heaped."
Still his white beard he tears, and his eyes weep.
Duke Naimès says : " His wrath is great indeed."

CCXI

2945 " Sire, Emperour," Gefrei d'Anjou implored,
" Let not your grief to such excess be wrought ;
Bid that our men through all this field be sought,
Whom those of Spain have in the battle caught ;
In a charnel command that they be borne."
2950 Answered the King : " Sound then upon your
horn."

CCXII

Gefreid d'Anjou upon his trumpet sounds ;
As Charlès bade them, all the Franks dismount.
All of their friends, whose bodies they have found
To a charnel speedily they bring down.
2955 Bishops there are, and abbots there enow,
Canons and monks, vicars with shaven crowns ;
Absolution in God's name they've pronounced ;
Incense and myrrh with precious gums they've
ground,
And lustily they've swung the censers round ;
2960 With honour great they've laid them in the
ground.
They've left them there ; what else might they
do now ?

CCXIII

That Emperour sets Rollant on one side
And Oliver, and the Archbishop Turpine ;
Their bodies bids open before his eyes
2965 And all their hearts in silken veils to wind,
And set them in coffers of marble white ;

After, they take the bodies of those knights,
Each of the three is wrapped in a deer's hide ;
They're washen well in allspice and in wine.
2970 The King commands Tedbalt and Gebuin,
Marquis Otun, Milun the count besides :
Along the road in three wagons to drive.
They're covered well with carpets Galazine.

CCXIV

Now to be off would that Emperour Charles,
2975 When pagans, lo ! comes surging the vanguard ;
Two messengers come from their ranks forward,
From the admiral bring challenge to combat :
" 'Tis not yet time, proud King, that thou de-
      part.
Lo, Baligant comes cantering afterward,
2980 Great are the hosts he leads from Arab parts ;
This day we'll see if thou hast vassalage."
Charlès the King his snowy beard has clasped,
Remembering his sorrow and damage,
Haughtily then his people all regards,
2985 In a loud voice he cries with all his heart :
" Barons and Franks, to horse, I say, to arms ! "

CCXV

First before all was armed that Emperour,
Nimbly enough his iron sark indued,
Laced up his helm, girt on his sword Joiuse,
2990 Outshone the sun that dazzling light it threw,
Hung from his neck a shield, was of Girunde,
And took his spear, was fashioned at Blandune.
On his good horse then mounted, Tencendur,
Which he had won at th'ford below Marsune
2995 When he flung dead Malpalin of Nerbune,
Let go the reins, spurred him with either foot ;
Five score thousand behind him as he flew,
Calling on God and the Apostle of Roum.

Through all the field dismount the Frankish men,
3000 Five-score thousand and more, they arm themselves ;
The gear they have enhances much their strength,
Their horses swift, their arms are fashioned well ;
Mounted they are, and fight with great science.
Find they that host, battle they'll render them.
3005 Their gonfalons flutter above their helms.
When Charlès sees the fair aspect of them,
He calls to him Jozeran of Provence,
Naimon the Duke, with Antelme of Maience :
" In such vassals should man have confidence,
3010 Whom not to trust were surely want of sense ;
Unless the Arabs of coming here repent,
Then Rollant's life, I think, we'll dearly sell."
Answers Duke Neimes : " God grant us His consent ! "

CCXVII

Charlès hath called Rabel and Guineman ;
3015 Thus said the King : " My lords, you I command
To take their place, Olivier's and Rollant's,
One bear the sword and the other the olifant ;
So canter forth ahead, before the van,
And in your train take fifteen thousand Franks,
3020 Young bachelors, that are most valiant.
As many more shall after them advance,
Whom Gebuins shall lead, also Lorains."
Naimès the Duke and the count Jozerans
Go to adjust these columns in their ranks.
3025 Find they that host, they'll make a grand attack.

CCXVIII

Of Franks the first columns made ready there,
After those two a third they next prepare ;
In it are set the vassals of Baiviere,
Some thousand score high-prizèd chevaliers ;

3030 Never was lost the battle, where they were ;
Charles for no race neath heaven hath more care,
Save those of France, who realms for him con-
quered.
The Danish chief, the warrior count Oger,
Shall lead that troop, for haughty is their air.

CCXIX

3035 Three columns now, he has, the Emperour
Charles.
Naimès the Duke a fourth next sets apart
Of good barons, endowed with vassalage ;
Germans they are, come from the German
March,
A thousand score, as all said afterward ;
3040 They're well equipped with horses and with
arms,
Rather they'll die than from the battle pass ;
They shall be led by Hermans, Duke of Trace,
Who'll die before he's any way coward.

CCXX

Naimès the Duke and the count Jozerans
3045 The fifth column have mustered, of Normans,
A thousand score, or so say all the Franks ;
Well armed are they, their horses charge and
prance ;
Rather they'ld die, than e'er be recreant ;
No race neath heav'n can more in th'field
compass.
3050 Richard the old, lead them in th'field he shall,
He'll strike hard there with his good trenchant
lance.

CCXXI

The sixth column is mustered of Bretons ;
Thirty thousand chevaliers therein come ;
These canter in the manner of barons,
3055 Upright their spears, their ensigns fastened on.

The overlord of them is named Oedon,
Who doth command the county Nevelon,
Tedbald of Reims and the marquis Oton :
" Lead ye my men, by my commission."

CCXXII

3060 That Emperour hath now six columns yare.
Naimès the Duke the seventh next prepares
Of Peitevins and barons from Alverne ;
Forty thousand chevaliers might be there ;
Their horses good, their arms are all most fair.
3065 They're neath a cliff, in a vale by themselves ;
With his right hand King Charlès hath them
blessed,
Them Jozerans shall lead, also Godselmes.

CCXXIII

And the eighth column hath Naimès made ready;
'Tis of Flamengs, and barons out of Frise ;
3070 Forty thousand and more good knights are these,
Nor lost by them has any battle been.
And the King says : " These shall do my ser-
vice."
Between Rembalt and Hamon of Galice
Shall they be led, for all their chivalry.

CCXXIV

3075 Between Naimon and Jozeran the count
Are prudent men for the ninth column found,
Of Lotherengs and those out of Borgoune ;
Fifty thousand good knights they are, by count ;
In helmets laced and sarks of iron brown,
3080 Strong are their spears, short are the shafts cut
down ;
If the Arrabits demur not, but come out
And trust themselves to these, they'll strike them
down.
Tierris the Duke shall lead them, of Argoune.

CCXXV

The tenth column is of barons of France,
Five score thousand of our best capitans ;
3085   Lusty of limb, and proud of countenance,
Snowy their heads are, and their beards are
    blanched,
In doubled sarks, and in hauberks they're clad,
Girt on their sides Frankish and Spanish brands
3090   And noble shields of divers cognisance.
Soon as they mount, the battle they demand,
" Monjoie " they cry. With them goes Charle-
    magne.
Gefreid d'Anjou carries that oriflamme ;
Saint Peter's 'twas, and bare the name Roman,
3095   But on that day Monjoie, by change, it gat.

CCXXVI

That Emperour down from his horse descends ;
To the green grass, kneeling, his face he bends.
Then turns his eyes towards the Orient,
Calls upon God with heartiest intent :
3100   " Very Father, this day do me defend,
Who to Jonas succour didst truly send
Out of the whale's belly, where he was pent ;
And who didst spare the king of Niniven,
And Daniel from marvellous torment
3105   When he was caged within the lions' den ;
And three children, all in a fire ardent :
Thy gracious Love to me be here present.
In Thy Mercy, if it please Thee, consent
That my nephew Rollant I may avenge."
3110   When he had prayed, upon his feet he stepped.
With the strong mark of virtue signed his head ;
Upon his swift charger the King mounted
While Jozerans and Neimes his stirrup held ;
He took his shield, his trenchant spear he kept ;
3115   Fine limbs he had, both gallant and well set ;
Clear was his face and filled with good intent.
Vigorously he cantered onward thence.

100

In front, in rear, they sounded their trumpets,
Above them all boomed the olifant again.
3120 Then all the Franks for pity of Rollant wept.

CCXXVII

That Emperour canters in noble array,
Over his sark all of his beard displays ;
For love of him, all others do the same,
Five score thousand Franks are thereby made
    plain.
3125 They pass those peaks, those rocks and those
    mountains,
Those terrible narrows, and those deep vales,
Then issue from the passes and the wastes
Till they are come into the March of Spain ;
A halt they've made, in th'middle of a plain.
3130 To Baligant his vanguard comes again,
A Sulian hath told him his message :
" We have seen Charles, that haughty sovereign ;
Fierce are his men, they have no mind to fail.
Arm yourself then : Battle you'll have to-day."
3135 Says Baligant : " Mine is great vassalage ;
Let horns this news to my pagans proclaim."

CCXXVIII

Through all the host they have their drums
    sounded,
And their bugles, and very clear trumpets.
Pagans dismount, that they may arm themselves.
3140 Their admiral will stay no longer then ;
Puts on a sark, embroidered in the hems,
Laces his helm, that is with gold begemmed ;
After, his sword on his left side he's set,
Out of his pride a name for it he's spelt
3145 Like to Carlun's, as he has heard it said,
So Preciuse he bad his own be clept ;
'Twas their ensign when they to battle went,
His chevaliers' ; he gave that cry to them.

His own broad shield he hangs upon his neck,
3150 (Round its gold boss a band of crystal went,
The strap of it was a good silken web) ;
He grasps his spear, the which he calls Maltet ;—
So great its shaft as is a stout cudgel,
Beneath its steel alone, a mule had bent ;
3155 On his charger is Baligant mounted,
Marcules, from over seas, his stirrup held.
That warrior, with a great stride he stepped,
Small were his thighs, his ribs of wide extent,
Great was his breast, and finely fashionèd,
3160 With shoulders broad and very clear aspect ;
Proud was his face, his hair was ringleted,
White as a flow'r in summer was his head.
His vassalage had often been provèd.
God ! what a knight, were he a Christian yet !
3165 His horse he's spurred, the clear blood issuèd ;
He's gallopped on, over a ditch he's leapt,
Full fifty feet a man might mark its breadth.
Pagans cry out : " Our Marches shall be held ;
There is no Frank, may once with him contest,
3170 Will he or nill, his life he'll soon have spent.
Charlès is mad, that he departs not hence."

CCXXIX

That admiral to a baron's like enough,
White is his beard as flow'rs by summer burnt ;
In his own laws, of wisdom hath he much ;
3175 And in battle he's proud and arduous.
His son Malprimes is very chivalrous,
He's great and strong ;—his ancestors were thus.
Says to his sire : " To canter then let us !
I marvel much that soon we'll see Carlun."
3180 Says Baligant : " Yea, for he's very pruff ;
In many tales honour to him is done ;
He hath no more Rollant, his sister's son,
He'll have no strength to stay in fight with us."

CCXXX

"Fair son Malprimes," then says t' him Baligant,
"Was slain yestre'en the good vassal Rollanz,
And Oliver, the proof and valiant,
The dozen peers, whom Charles so cherished,
    and
Twenty thousand more Frankish combatants.
For all the rest I'ld not unglove my hand.
But the Emperour is verily come back,
—So tells me now my man, that Sulian—
Ten great columns, he's set them in their ranks ;
He's a proof man who sounds that olifant,
With a clear call he rallies his comrades ;
These at the head come cantering in advance,
Also with them are fifteen thousand Franks,
Young bachelors, whom Charlès calls Infants ;
As many again come following that band,
Who will lay on with utmost arrogance."
Then says Malprimes : "The first blow I de-
    mand."

CCXXXI

"Fair son Malprimes," says Baligant to him,
"I grant it you, as you have asked me this ;
Against the Franks go now, and smite them quick.
And take with you Torleu, the Persian king
And Dapamort, another king Leutish.
Their arrogance if you can humble it,
Of my domains a slice to you I'll give
From Cheriant unto the Vale Marquis."
"I thank you, Sire !" Malprimès answers him ;
Going before, he takes delivery ;
'Tis of that land, was held by king Flurit.
After that hour he never looked on it,
Investiture gat never, nor seizin.

CCXXXII

That admiral canters among his hosts ;
After, his son with's great body follows,

Torleus the king, and the king Dapamort ;
Thirty columns most speedily they form.
They've chevaliers in marvellous great force ;
Fifty thousand the smallest column holds.
3220 The first is raised of men from Butenrot,
The next, after, Micenes, whose heads are gross ;
Along their backs, above their spinal bones,
As they were hogs, great bristles on them grow.
The third is raised from Nubles and from Blos ;
The fourth is raised from Bruns and Esclavoz ;
3225 The fifth is raised from Sorbres and from Sorz;
The sixth is raised from Ermines and from Mors ;
The seventh is the men of Jericho ;
Negroes are the eighth ; the ninth are men of
      Gros ;
3230 The tenth is raised from Balide the stronghold
That is a tribe no goodwill ever shews.
That admiral hath sworn, the way he knows,
By Mahumet, his virtues and his bones :
" Charlès of France is mad to canter so ;
3235 Battle he'll have, unless he take him home ;
No more he'll wear on's head that crown of gold."

CCXXXIII

Ten great columns they marshal thereafter :
Of Canelious, right ugly, is the first,
Who from Val-Fuit came across country there;
3240 The next's of Turks ; of Persians is the third ;
The fourth is raised of desperate Pinceners,
The fifth is raised from Soltras and Avers ;
The sixth is from Ormaleus and Eugez ;
The seventh is the tribe of Samuel ;
3245 The eighth is from Bruise ; the ninth from
      Esclavers ;
The tenth is from Occiant, the desert,
That is a tribe, do not the Lord God serve,
Of such felons you never else have heard ;
Hard is their hide, as though it iron were,
3250 Wherefore of helm or hauberk they've no care ;
In the battle they're felon murderers.

That admiral ten columns more reviews;
The first is raised of Giants from Malpruse;
The next of Huns; the third a Hungar crew;
255 And from Baldise the Long the fourth have
    trooped;
The fifth is raised of men from Val-Penuse;
The sixth is raised of tribesmen from Maruse;
The seventh is from Leus and Astrimunes;
The eighth from Argoilles; the ninth is from
    Clarbune;
260 The tenth is raised of beardsmen from Val-
    Frunde,
That is a tribe, no love of God e'er knew.
Gesta Francor' these thirty columns prove.
Great are the hosts, their horns come sounding
    through.
Pagans canter as men of valour should.

CCXXXV

3265 That admiral hath great possessions;
He makes them bear before him his dragon,
And their standard, Tervagan's and Mahom's,
And his image, Apollin the felon.
Ten Canelious canter in the environs,
3270 And very loud they cry out this sermon:
" Let who would from our gods have garrison,
Serve them and pray with great affliction."
Pagans awhile their heads and faces on
Their breasts abase, their polished helmets doff.
3275 And the Franks say: " Now shall you die,
    gluttons;
This day shall bring you vile confusion!
Give warranty, our God, unto Carlon!
And in his name this victory be won!"

CCXXXVI

That admiral hath wisdom great indeed;
3280 His son to him and those two kings calls he:

"My lords barons, beforehand canter ye,
All my columns together shall you lead ;
But of the best I'll keep beside me three :
One is of Turks ; the next of Ormaleis ;
3285   And the third is the Giants of Malpreis.
And Occiant's, they'll also stay with me,
Until with Charles and with the Franks they
    meet.
That Emperour, if he combat with me,
Must lose his head, cut from his shoulders clean ;
3290   He may be sure naught else for him's decreed."

CCXXXVII

Great are the hosts, and all the columns fair,
No peak nor vale nor cliff between them there,
Thicket nor wood, nor ambush anywhere ;
Across the plain they see each other well.
3295   Says Baligant : " My pagan tribes adverse,
Battle to seek, canter ye now ahead ! "
Carries the ensign Amboires of Oluferne ;
Pagans cry out, by Preciuse they swear.
And the Franks say : " Great hurt this day you'll
    get ! "
3300   And very loud " Monjoie ! " they cry again.
That Emperour has bid them sound trumpets ;
And the olifant sounds over all its knell.
The pagans say : " Carlun's people are fair.
Battle we'll have, bitter and keenly set."

CCXXXVIII

3305   Great is that plain, and wide is that country ;
Their helmets shine with golden jewelry,
Also their sarks embroidered and their shields,
And the ensigns fixed on all their burnished
    spears.
The trumpets sound, their voice is very clear,
3310   And the olifant its echoing music speaks.
Then the admiral, his brother calleth he,
'Tis Canabeus, the king of Floredee,

Who holds the land unto the Vale Sevree ;
He's shewn to him Carlun's ten companies :
3315 " The pride of France, renownèd land, you see.
That Emperour canters right haughtily,
His bearded men are with him in the rear ;
Over their sarks they have thrown out their
    beards
Which are as white as driven snows that freeze.
3320 Strike us they will with lances and with spears :
Battle with them we'll have, prolonged and
    keen ;
Never has man beheld such armies meet."
Further than one might cast a rod that's peeled
Goes Baligant before his companies.
3325 His reason then he's shewn to them, and speaks :
" Pagans, come on ; for now I take the field."
His spear in hand he brandishes and wields,
Towards Carlun has turned the point of steel.

CCXXXIX

Charlès the Great, when he sees the admiral
3330 And the dragon, his ensign and standard ;—
(In such great strength are mustered those Arabs
Of that country they've covered every part
Save only that whereon the Emperour was.)
The King of France in a loud voice has called :
3335 " Barons and Franks, good vassals are ye all,
Ye in the field have fought so great combats ;
See the pagans ; they're felons and cowards,
No pennyworth is there in all their laws.
Though they've great hosts, my lords, what
    matters that ?
3340 Let him go hence, who'ld fail me in the attack."
Next with both spurs he's gored his horse's
    flanks,
And Tencendor has made four bounds thereat.
Then say the Franks : " This King's a good
    vassal.
Canter, brave lord, for none of us holds back."

CCXL

3345 Clear is the day, and the sun radiant ;
The hosts are fair, the companies are grand.
The first columns are come now hand to hand.
The count Rabel and the count Guinemans
Let fall the reins on their swift horses' backs,
3350 Spurring in haste ; then on rush all the Franks,
And go to strike, each with his trenchant lance.

CCXLI

That count Rabel, he was a hardy knight,
He pricked his horse with spurs of gold so fine,
The Persian king, Torleu, he went to strike.
3355 Nor shield nor sark could such a blow abide ;
The golden spear his carcass passed inside ;
Flung down upon a little bush, he died.
Then say the Franks : " Lord God, be Thou
      our Guide !
Charlès we must not fail ; his cause is right."

CCXLII

3360 And Guineman tilts with the king Leutice ;
Has broken all the flowers on his shield,
Next of his sark he has undone the seam,
All his ensign thrust through the carcass clean,
So flings him dead, let any laugh or weep.
3365 Upon that blow, the Franks cry out with heat :
" Strike on, baron, nor slacken in your speed !
Charle's in the right against the pagan breed ;
God sent us here his justice to complete."

CCXLIII

Pure white the horse whereon Malprimès sate ;
3370 Guided his corse amid the press of Franks,
Hour in, hour out, great blows he struck them
      back,
And, ever, dead one upon others packed.
Before them all has cried out Baligant :
" Barons, long time I've fed you at my hand.

3375 Ye see my son, who goes on Carlun's track,
And with his arms so many lords attacks ;
Better vassal than him I'll not demand.
Go, succour him, each with his trenchant lance !"
Upon that word the pagans all advance ;
3380 Grim blows they strike, the slaughter's very
grand.
And marvellous and weighty the combat :
Before nor since was never such attack.

CCXLIV

Great are the hosts ; the companies in pride
Come touching, all the breadth of either side ;
3385 And the pagans do marvellously strike.
So many shafts, by God ! in pieces lie,
And crumpled shields, and sarks with mail un-
twined !
So spattered all the earth there would you find
That through the field the grass so green and fine
3390 With men's life-blood is all vermilion dyed.
That admiral rallies once more his tribe :
" Barons, strike on, shatter the Christian line."
Now very keen and lasting is the fight,
As never was, before or since that time ;
3395 The finish none shall reach, unless he die.

CCXLV

That admiral to all his race appeals :
" Pagans, strike on ; came you not therefore here ?
I promise you noble women and dear,
I promise you honours and lands and fiefs."
3400 Answer pagans : " We must do well indeed.'
With mighty blows they shatter all their spears ;
Five score thousand swords from their scabbards
leap,
Slaughter then, grim and sorrowful, you'd seen.
Battle he saw, that stood those hosts between.

CCXLVI

3405 That Emperour calls on his Franks and speaks :
" I love you, lords, in whom I well believe ;
So many great battles you've fought for me,
Kings overthrown, and kingdoms have redeemed!
Guerdon I owe, I know it well indeed ;
3410 My lands, my wealth, my body are yours to keep.
Vengeance for sons, for heirs, for brothers wreak
Who in Rencesvals were slaughtered yester-eve !
Mine is the right, ye know, gainst pagan breeds."
Answer the Franks : " Sire, 'tis the truth you
speak."
3415 Twenty thousand beside him Charlès leads,
Who with one voice have sworn him fealty ;
In straits of death they never will him leave.
There is not one thenceforth employs his spear,
But with their swords they strike in company.
3420 The battle is straitened marvellously.

CCXLVII

Across that field the bold Malprimès canters ;
Who of the Franks hath wrought there much
great damage.
Naimès the Duke right haughtily regards him,
And goes to strike him, like a man of valour,
3425 And of his shield breaks all the upper margin,
Tears both the sides of his embroidered ha'berk,
Through the carcass thrusts all his yellow banner;
So dead among sev'n hundred else he casts him.

CCXLVIII

King Canabeus, brother of the admiral,
3430 Has pricked his horse with spurs in either flank ;
He's drawn his sword, whose hilt is of crystal,
And strikes Naimun on's helmet principal ;
Away from it he's broken off one half,
Five of the links his brand of steel hath knapped;
3435 No pennyworth the hood is after that ;
Right to the flesh he slices through the cap :

The folds of his hauberk apart he slashed,
Two of his ribs out of his side he hacked,
So flung him dead, while still his charger ran.
After, he slew Gebuin and Lorain,
3470 Richard the old, the lord of those Normans.
" Preciuse," cry pagans, " is valiant !
Baron, strike on ; here have we our warrant ! "

CCLII

Who then had seen those Arrabit chevaliers,
From Occiant, from Argoille and from Bascle !
3475 And well they strike and slaughter with their
lances ;
But Franks, to escape they think it no great
matter ;
On either side dead men to the earth fall crash-
ing.
Till even-tide 'tis very strong, that battle ;
Barons of France do suffer much great damage,
3480 Grief shall be there ere the two hosts be scattered.

CCLIII

Right well they strike, both Franks and Arrabies,
Breaking the shafts of all their burnished spears.
Whoso had seen that shattering of shields,
Whoso had heard those shining hauberks creak,
3485 And heard those shields on iron helmets beat,
Whoso had seen fall down those chevaliers,
And heard men groan, dying upon that field,
Some memory of bitter pains might keep.
That battle is most hard to endure, indeed.
3490 And the admiral calls upon Apollin
And Tervagant and Mahum, prays and speaks :
" My lords and gods, I've done you much ser-
vice ;
Your images, in gold I'll fashion each :
Against Carlun give me your warranty ! "
3495 Comes before him his dear friend Gemalfin,
Evil the news he brings to him and speaks :

One piece of it he's flung upon the land.
Great was the blow ; the Duke, amazed thereat,
Had fallen ev'n, but aid from God he had ;
His charger's neck he clasped with both his
    hands.
Had the pagan but once renewed the attack,
Then was he slain, that noble old vassal.
Came there to him, with succour, Charles of
    France.

CCXLIX

Keen anguish then he suffers, that Duke Naimès,
And the pagan, to strike him, hotly hastens.
" Culvert," says Charles, " You'll get now as
    you gave him ! "
With vassalage he goes to strike that pagan,
Shatters his shield, against his heart he breaks it,
Tears the chin-guard above his hauberk mailèd ;
So flings him dead : his saddle shall be wasted.

CCL

Bitter great grief has Charlemagne the King,
Who Duke Naimun before him sees lying,
On the green grass all his clear blood shedding.
Then the Emperour to him this counsel gives :
" Fair master Naimes, canter with me to win !
The glutton's dead, that had you straitly pinned ;
Through his carcass my spear I thrust once in."
Answers the Duke : " Sire, I believe it, this.
Great proof you'll have of valour, if I live."
They 'ngage them then, true love and faith swear-
    ing ;
A thousand score of Franks surround them still.
Nor is there one, but slaughters, strikes and kills.

CCLI

Then through the field cantered that admiral,
Going to strike the county Guineman ;
Against his heart his argent shield he cracked,

3440

3445

3450

3455

3460

3465

" Sir Baliganz, this day in shame you're steeped;
For you have lost your son, even Malprime ;
And Canabeus, your brother, slain is he.
3500 Fairly two Franks have got the victory ;
That Emperour was one, as I have seen ;
Great limbs he has, he's every way Marquis,
White is his beard as flowers in April."
505 That admiral has bent his head down deep,
And thereafter lowers his face and weeps,
Fain would he die at once, so great his grief ;
He calls to him Jangleu from over sea.

CCLIV

Says the admiral : " Jangleu, beside me stand !
For you are proof, and greatly understand,
3510 Counsel from you I've ever sought to have.
How seems it you, of Arrabits and Franks,
Shall we from hence victorious go back ? "
He answers him : " Slain are you, Baligant !
For from your gods you'll never have warrant.
3515 So proud is Charles, his men so valiant,
Never saw I a race so combatant.
But call upon barons of Occiant,
Turks and Enfruns, Arrabits and Giants.
No more delay : what must be, take in hand."

CCLV

3520 That admiral has shaken out his beard
That ev'n so white as thorn in blossom seems ;
He'll no way hide, whate'er his fate may be,
Then to his mouth he sets a trumpet clear,
And clearly sounds, so all the pagans hear.
3525 Throughout the field rally his companies.
From Occiant, those men who bray and bleat,
And from Argoille, who, like dogs barking, speak ;
Seek out the Franks with such a high folly,
Break through their line, the thickest press they
    meet
3530 Dead from that shock they've seven thousand
    heaped.

The count Oger no cowardice e'er knew,
Better vassal hath not his sark indued.
He sees the Franks, their columns broken through,
So calls to him Duke Tierris, of Argune,
3535 Count Jozeran, and Gefreid, of Anjou ;
And to Carlun most proud his reason proves :
" Behold pagans, and how your men they slew !
Now from your head please God the crown remove
Unless you strike, and vengeance on them do ! "
3540 And not one word to answer him he knew ;
They spurred in haste, their horses let run loose,
And, wheresoe'er they met the pagans, strook.

CCLVII

Now very well strikes the King Charlemain,
Naimès the Duke, Oger also, the Dane,
3545 Geifreid d'Anjou, who that ensign displays.
Exceeding proof is Don Oger, the Dane ;
He spurs his horse, and lets him run in haste,
So strikes that man who the dragon displays ;
Both in the field before his feet he breaks
3550 That king's ensign and dragon, both abased.
Baligant sees his gonfalon disgraced,
And Mahumet's standard thrown from its place;
That admiral at once perceives it plain,
That he is wrong, and right is Charlemain.
3555 Pagan Arabs coyly themselves contain ;
That Emperour calls on his Franks again :
" Say, barons, come, support me, in God's
Name ! "
Answer the Franks : " Question you make in vain ;
All felon he that dares not exploits brave ! "

CCLVIII

3560 Passes that day, turns into vesper-tide.
Franks and pagans still with their swords do
strike.

Brave vassals they, who brought those hosts to
    fight,
Never have they forgotten their ensigns ;
That admiral still " Preciuse " doth cry,
3565   Charlès " Monjoie," renownèd word of pride.
Each the other knows by his clear voice and
    high ;
Amid the field they're both come into sight,
Then, as they go, great blows on either side
They with their spears on their round targes
    strike ;
3570   And shatter them, beneath their buckles wide ;
And all the folds of their hauberks divide ;
But bodies, no ; wound them they never might.
Broken their girths, downwards their saddles
    slide ;
Both those Kings fall, themselves aground do
    find ;
3575   Nimbly enough upon their feet they rise ;
Most vassal-like they draw their swords outright.
From this battle they'll ne'er be turned aside
Nor make an end, without that one man die.

CCLIX

A great vassal was Charles, of France the Douce ;
3580   That admiral no fear nor caution knew.
Those swords they had, bare from their sheaths
    they drew ;
Many great blows on 's shield each gave and took ;
The leather pierced, and doubled core of wood ;
Down fell the nails, the buckles brake in two ;
3585   Still they struck on, bare in their sarks they
    stood.
From their bright helms the light shone forth
    anew.
Finish nor fail that battle never could
But one of them must in the wrong be proved.

CCLX

3590 Says the admiral : " Nay, Charlès, think, I beg,
And counsel take that t'wards me thou repent !
Thou'st slain my son, I know that very well ;
Most wrongfully my land thou challengest ;
Become my man, a fief from me thou'lt get ;
Come, serving me, from here to the Orient ! "
3595 Charle answers him : " That were most vile
offence ;
No peace nor love may I to pagan lend.
Receive the Law that God to us presents,
Christianity, and then I'll love thee well ;
Serve and believe the King Omnipotent ! "
3600 Says Baligant : " Evil sermon thou saist."
They go to strike with th'swords, are on their
belts.

CCLXI

In the admiral is much great virtue found ;
He strikes Carlun on his steel helm so brown,
Has broken it and rent, above his brow,
3605 Through his thick hair the sword goes glancing
round,
A great palm's breadth and more of flesh cuts
out,
So that all bare the bone is, in that wound.
Charles tottereth, falls nearly to the ground ;
God wills not he be slain or overpow'red.
3610 Saint Gabriel once more to him comes down,
And questions him : " Great King, what doest
thou ? "

CCLXII

Charles, hearing how that holy Angel spake,
Had fear of death no longer, nor dismay ;
Remembrance and a fresh vigour he's gained.
3615 So the admiral he strikes with France's blade,
His helmet breaks, whereon the jewels blaze,
Slices his head, to scatter all his brains,

And, down unto the white beard, all his face ;
So he falls dead, recovers not again.
3620 " Monjoie," cries Charles, that all may know the
            tale.
Upon that word is come to him Duke Naimes,
Holds Tencendur, bids mount that King so
        Great.
Pagans turn back, God wills not they remain.
And Franks have all their wish, be that what
        may.

CCLXIII

3625 Pagans are fled, ev'n as the Lord God wills ;
Chase them the Franks, and the Emperour there-
        with.
Says the King then : " My Lords, avenge your
        ills,
Unto your hearts' content, do what you will !
For tears, this morn, I saw your eyes did spill."
3630 Answer the Franks : " Sir, even so we will."
Then such great blows, as each may strike, he
        gives
That few escape, of those remain there still.

CCLXIV

Great was the heat, the dust arose and blew ;
Still pagans fled, and hotly Franks pursued.
3635 The chase endured from there to Sarraguce.
On her tower, high up clomb Bramimunde,
Around her there the clerks and canons stood
Of the false law, whom God ne'er loved nor knew;
Orders they'd none, nor were their heads ton-
        sured.
3640 And when she saw those Arrabits confused
Aloud she cried : " Give us your aid, Mahume!"
Ah ! Noble king, conquered are all our troops,
And the admiral to shameful slaughter put ! "
When Marsile heard, towards the wall he looked,
3645 Wept from his eyes, and all his body stooped,
So died of grief. With sins he's so corrupt,
The soul of him to Hell live devils took.

CCLXV

Pagans are slain ; the rest are put to rout
Whom Charlès hath in battle overpow'red.
3650   Of Sarraguce the gates he's battered down,
For well he knows there's no defence there now ;
In come his men, he occupies that town ;
And all that night they lie there in their pow'r.
Fierce is that King, with 's hoary beard, and
     proud,
3655   And Bramimunde hath yielded up her tow'rs ;—
But ten were great, and lesser fifty around.
Great exploits his whom the Lord God endows !

CCLXVI

Passes the day, the darkness is grown deep,
But all the stars burn, and the moon shines clear.
3660   And Sarraguce is in the Emperour's keep.
A thousand Franks he bids seek through the
     streets,
The synagogues and the mahumeries ;
With iron malls and axes which they wield
They break the idols and all the imageries ;
3665   So there remain no fraud nor falsity.
That King fears God, and would do His service;
On water then Bishops their blessing speak,
And pagans bring into the baptistry.
If any Charles with contradiction meet
3670   Then hanged or burned or slaughtered shall he
     be.
Five score thousand and more are thus redeemed,
Very Christians ; save that alone the queen
To France the Douce goes in captivity :
By love the King will her conversion seek.

CCLXVII

3675   Passes the night, the clear day opens now.
Of Sarraguce Charles garrisons the tow'rs ;
A thousand knights he's left there, fighters stout;
Who guard that town as bids their Emperour.

3680 After, the King and all his army mount,
And Bramimunde a prisoner is bound,
No harm to her, but only good he's vowed.
So are they come, with joy and gladness out,
They pass Nerbone by force and by vigour,
Come to Burdele, that city of high valour.

3685 Above the altar, to Saint Sevrin endowed,
Stands the olifant, with golden pieces bound;
All the pilgrims may see it, who thither crowd.
Passing Girunde, in ships that there abound,
Ev'n unto Blaive he's brought his nephew down

3690 And Oliver, his noble companioun,
And the Archbishop, who was so wise and
proud.
In white coffers he bids them lay those counts
At Saint Romain : So rest they in that ground.
Franks them to God and to His Angels vow.

3695 Charles canters on, by valleys and by mounts,
Not before Aix will he not make sojourn;
Canters so far, on th'terrace he dismounts.
When he is come into his lofty house,
By messengers he seeks his judges out;

3700 Saxons, Baivers, Lotherencs and Frisouns,
Germans he calls, and also calls Borgounds;
From Normandy, from Brittany and Poitou,
And those in France that are the sagest found.
Thereon begins the cause of Gueneloun.

CCLXVIII

3705 That Emperour, returning out of Spain,
Arrived in France, in his chief seat, at Aix,
Clomb to th' Palace, into the hall he came.
Was come to him there Alde, that fair dame;
Said to the King : " Where's Rollanz the Cap-
tain,

3710 Who sware to me, he'ld have me for his mate ? "
Then upon Charles a heavy sorrow weighed,
And his eyes wept, he tore his beard again :
" Sister, dear friend, of a dead man you spake.
I'll give you one far better in exchange,

119

3715 That is Loewis, what further can I say ;
He is my son, and shall my marches take."
Alde answered him : " That word to me is
        strange.
Never, please God, His Angels and His Saints,
When Rollant's dead shall I alive remain ! "
3720 Her colour fails, at th' feet of Charlemain
She falls ; she's dead. Her soul God's Mercy
        awaits !
Barons of France weep therefore and complain.

CCLXIX

Alde the fair is gone now to her rest.
Yet the King thought she was but swooning then,
3725 Pity he had, our Emperour, and wept,
Took her in's hands, raised her from th'earth
        again ;
On her shoulders her head still drooped and leant.
When Charlès saw that she was truly dead
Four countesses at once he summonèd ;
3730 To a monast'ry of nuns they bare her thence,
All night their watch until the dawn they held ;
Before the altar her tomb was fashioned well ;
Her memory the King with honour kept.

CCLXX

That Emperour is now returned to Aix.
3735 The felon Guene, all in his iron chains
Is in that town, before the King's Palace ;
Those serfs have bound him, fast upon his stake,
In deer-hide thongs his hands they've helpless
        made,
With clubs and whips they trounce him well and
        baste :
3740 He has deserved not any better fate ;
In bitter grief his trial there he awaits.

CCLXXI

Written it is, and in an ancient geste
How Charlès called from many lands his men,

Assembled them at Aix, in his Chapelle.
3745 Holy that day, for some chief feast was held,
Saint Silvester's that baron's, many tell.
Thereon began the trial and defence
Of Guenelun, who had the treason spelt.
Before himself the Emperour has him led.

CCLXXII

3750 " Lords and barons," Charlès the King doth
        speak,
" Of Guenelun judge what the right may be !
He was in th'host, even in Spain with me ;
There of my Franks a thousand score did steal,
And my nephew, whom never more you'll see,
3755 And Oliver, in 's pride and courtesy,
And, wealth to gain, betrayed the dozen peers."
" Felon be I," said Guenes, " aught to conceal !
He did from me much gold and wealth forfeit,
Whence to destroy and slay him did I seek ;
3760 But treason, no ; I vow there's not the least."
Answer the Franks : " Take counsel now must
        we."

CCLXXIII

So Guenelun, before the King there, stood ;
Lusty his limbs, his face of gentle hue ;
Were he loyal, right baron-like he'd looked.
3765 He saw those Franks, and all who'ld judge his
        doom,
And by his side his thirty kinsmen knew.
After, he cried aloud ; his voice was full :
" For Love of God, listen to me, baruns !
I was in th' host, beside our Emperour,
3770 Service I did him there in faith and truth.
Hatred of me had Rollant, his nephew ;
So he decreed death for me and dolour.
Message I bare to king Marsiliun ;
By my cunning I held myself secure.
3775 To that fighter Rollant my challenge threw,
To Oliver, and all their comrades too ;

Charlès heard that, and his noble baruns.
Vengeance I gat, but there's no treason proved."
Answered the Franks : " Now go we to the
moot."

CCLXXIV

3780 When Guenès sees, his great cause is beginning,
Thirty he has around him of his kinsmen,
There's one of them to whom the others listen,
'Tis Pinabel, who in Sorence castle liveth ;
Well can he speak, soundly his reasons giving,
3785 A good vassal, whose arm to fight is stiffened
Says to him Guenes : " In you my faith is fixèd.
Save me this day from death, also from prison."
Says Pinabel : " Straightway you'll be de-
    livered.
Is there one Frank, that you to hang committeth?
3790 Let the Emperour but once together bring us,
With my steel brand he shall be smartly chidden."
Guenès the count kneels at his feet to kiss them.

CCLXXV

To th' counsel go those of Bavier and Saxe,
Normans also, with Poitevins and Franks ;
3795 Enough there are of Tudese and Germans.
Those of Alverne the greatest court'sy have,
From Pinabel most quietly draw back.
Says each to each : " 'Twere well to let it stand.
Leave we this cause, and of the King demand
3800 That he cry quits with Guenès for this act ;
With love and faith he'll serve him after that.
Since he is dead, no more ye'll see Rollanz,
Nor any wealth nor gold may win him back.
Most foolish then is he, would do combat."
3805 There is but one agrees not to their plan ;
Tierri, brother to Don Geifreit, 's that man.

CCLXXVI

Then his barons, returning to Carlun,
Say to their King : " Sire, we beseech of you

That you cry quits with county Guenelun,
3810   So he may serve you still in love and truth ;
Nay let him live, so noble a man 's he proved.
Rollant is dead, no longer in our view,
Nor for no wealth may we his life renew."
Then says the King : " You're felons all of
          you ! "

CCLXXVII

3815   When Charlès saw that all of them did fail,
Deep down he bowed his head and all his face ;
For th' grief he had, caitiff himself proclaimed.
One of his knights, Tierris, before him came,
Gefrei's brother, that Duke of Anjou famed ;
3820   Lean were his limbs, and lengthy and delicate,
Black was his hair and somewhat brown his face ;
Was not too small, and yet was hardly great ;
And courteously to the Emperour he spake :
" Fair Lord and King, do not yourself dismay !
3825   You know that I have served you many ways :
By my ancestors should I this cause maintain.
And if Rollant was forfeited to Guenes
Still your service to him full warrant gave.
Felon is Guene, since th' hour that he betrayed,
3830   And, towards you, is perjured and ashamed :
Wherefore I judge that he be hanged and slain,
His carcass flung to th' dogs beside the way,
As a felon who felony did make.
But, has he a friend that would dispute my claim
3835   With this my sword which I have girt in place
My judgement will I warrant every way."
Answer the Franks : " Now very well you spake."

CCLXXVIII

Before the King is come now Pinabel ;
Great is he, strong, vassalous and nimble ;
3840   Who bears his blow has no more time to dwell :
Says to him : " Sire, on you this cause depends ;
Command therefore this noise be made an end.
See Tierri here, who hath his judgment dealt ;

123

I cry him false, and will the cause contest."
3845 His deer-hide glove in the King's hand he's
left.
Says the Emperour : " Good pledges must I
get."
Thirty kinsmen offer their loyal pledge.
" I'll do the same for you," the King has said ;
Until the right be shewn, bids guard them well.

CCLXXIX

3850 When Tierri sees that battle shall come after,
His right hand glove he offereth to Charlès.
That Emperour by way of hostage guards it ;
Four benches then upon the place he marshals
Where sit them down champions of either party.
855 They're chos'n aright, as the others' judgement
cast them ;
Oger the Dane between them made the parley.
Next they demand their horses and their armour.

CCLXXX.

For battle, now, ready you might them see,
They're well confessed, absolved, from sin set
free ;
3860 Masses they've heard, Communion received,
Rich offerings to those minsters they leave.
Before Carlun now both the two appear :
They have their spurs, are fastened on their feet,
And light and strong, their hauberks brightly
gleam ;
3865 Upon their heads they've laced their helmets
clear,
And girt on swords, with pure gold hilted each ;
And from their necks hang down their quartered
shields ;
In their right hands they grasp their trenchant
spears.
At last they mount on their swift coursing steeds.
3870 Five score thousand chevaliers therefor weep,

For Rollant's sake pity for Tierri feel.
God knows full well which way the end shall be.

CCLXXXI

Down under Aix there is a pasture large
Which for the fight of th' two barons is marked.
3875 Proof men are these, and of great vassalage,
And their horses, unwearied, gallop fast ;
They spur them well, the reins aside they cast,
With virtue great, to strike each other, dart ;
All of their shields shatter and rend apart.
3880 Their hauberks tear ; the girths asunder start,
The saddles slip, and fall upon the grass.
Five score thousand weep, who that sight regard.

CCLXXXII

Upon the ground are fallen both the knights ;
Nimbly enough upon their feet they rise.
3885 Nimble and strong is Pinabels, and light.
Each the other seeks ; horses are out of mind,
But with those swords whose hilts with gold are
        lined
Upon those helms of steel they beat and strike :
Great are the blows, those helmets to divide.
3890 The chevaliers of France do much repine.
" O God ! " says Charles, " Make plain to us
        the right ! "

CCLXXXIII

Says Pinabel : " Tierri, I pray thee, yield :
I'll be thy man, in love and fealty ;
For thy pleasure my wealth I'll give to thee ;
3895 But make the King with Guenelun agree."
Answers Tierri : " Such counsel's not for me.
Pure felon I, if e'er I that concede !
God shall this day the right shew, us between ! "

CCLXXXIV

Then said Tierri: Bold art thou, Pinabel,
3900 Thou'rt great and strong, with body finely bred ;
For vassalage thy peers esteem thee well :
Of this battle let us now make an end !
With Charlemagne I soon will have thee friends ;
To Guenelun such justice shall be dealt
3905 Day shall not dawn but men of it will tell."
" Please the Lord God, not so ! " said Pinabel.
" I would sustain the cause of my kindred
No mortal man is there from whom I've fled ;
Rather I'ld die than hear reproaches said."
3910 Then with their swords began to strike again
Upon those helms that were with gold begemmed
Into the sky the bright sparks rained and fell.
It cannot be that they be sunderèd,
Nor make an end, without one man be dead.

CCLXXXV

3915 He's very proof, Pinabel of Sorence,
Tierri he strikes, on 's helmet of Provence,
Leaps such a spark, the grass is kindled thence ;
Of his steel brand the point he then presents,
On Tierri's brow the helmet has he wrenched
3920 So down his face its broken halves descend ;
And his right cheek in flowing blood is drenched;
And his hauberk, over his belly, rent.
God's his warrant, Who death from him prevents.

CCLXXXVI

Sees Tierris then that in the face he's struck,
3925 On grassy field runs clear his flowing blood ;
Strikes Pinabel on 's helmet brown and rough,
To the nose-piece he's broken it and cut,
And from his head scatters his brains in th' dust ;
Brandishes him on th' sword, till dead he's flung.
3930 Upon that blow is all the battle won.
Franks cry aloud : " God hath great virtue done.

It is proved right that Guenelun be hung
And those his kin, that in his cause are come."

CCLXXXVII

Now that Tierris the battle fairly wins,
3935   That Emperour Charlès is come to him ;
Forty barons are in his following,
Naimès the Duke, Oger that Danish Prince,
Geifrei d'Anjou, Willalme of Blaive therewith.
Tierri, the King takes in his arms to kiss ;
3940   And wipes his face with his great marten-skins ;
He lays them down, and others then they bring ;
The chevaliers most sweetly disarm him ;
An Arab mule they've brought, whereon he sits.
With baronage and joy they bring him in.
3945   They come to Aix, halt and dismount therein.
The punishment of the others then begins.

CCLXXXVIII

His counts and Dukes then calls to him Carlun ;
" With these I guard, advise what shall be done.
Hither they came because of Guenelun ;
3950   For Pinabel, as pledges gave them up."
Answer the Franks : " Shall not of them live
    one."
The King commands his provost then, Basbrun :
" Go hang them all on th' tree of cursèd wood !
Nay, by this beard, whose hairs are white enough,
3955   If one escape, to death and shame thou'rt struck !"
He answers him : " How could I act, save thus ?"
With an hundred serjeants by force they come ;
Thirty of them there are, that straight are hung.
Who betrays man, himself and 's friends undoes.

CCLXXXIX

3960   Then turned away the Baivers and Germans
And Poitevins and Bretons and Normans.
Fore all the rest, 'twas voted by the Franks

That Guenès die with marvellous great pangs.
So to lead forth four stallions they bade ;
3965 After, they bound his feet and both his hands ;
Those steeds were swift, and of a temper mad ;
Which, by their heads, led forward four serjeants
Towards a stream that flowed amid that land.
So Guenès fell into perdition black ;
3970 All his sinews were strained until they snapped,
And all the limbs were from his body dragged ;
On the green grass his clear blood gushed and
    ran.
Guenès is dead, a felon recreant.
Who betrays man, need make no boast of that.

CCXC

3975 When the Emperour had made his whole ven-
    geance,
He called to him the Bishops out of France,
Those of Baviere and also the Germans :
" A dame free-born lies captive in my hands,
So oft she's heard sermons and reprimands,
3980 She would fear God, and christening demands.
Baptise her then, so God her soul may have."
They answer him : " Sponsors the rite demands,
Dames of estate and long inheritance."
The baths at Aix great companies attract ;
3985 There they baptised the Queen of Sarazands,
And found for her the name of Juliane.
Christian is she by very cognisance.

CCXCI

When the Emperour his justice hath achieved,
His mighty wrath's abated from its heat,
3990 And Bramimunde has christening received ;
Passes the day, the darkness is grown deep,
And now that King in 's vaulted chamber sleeps.
Saint Gabriel is come from God, and speaks :
" Summon the hosts, Charlès, of thine Empire,
3995 Go thou by force into the land of Bire,

128

King Vivien thou'lt succour there, at Imphe,
In the city which pagans have besieged.
The Christians there implore thee and beseech."
Right loth to go, that Emperour was he:
4000 " God ! " said the King : " My life is hard in-
    deed ! "
Tears filled his eyes, he tore his snowy beard.

SO ENDS THE TALE
WHICH
TUROLD HATH CONCEIVED.

Translator's Note

WHAT follows is not a work of scholarship, nor yet of imagination : it is an attempt to reproduce line for line, and, so far as is possible, word for word, the Old French epic poem which lay dormant for centuries in the Bodleian Library at Oxford.

My part in it began almost by accident when, on a hot afternoon in the summer of 1918, turning into the coolness of Hatchard's, I found lying there a copy of M. Petit de Julleville's edition of *La Chanson de Roland*.* Amid the distractions of that summer in London, where the sound of the olifant came so often and so direfully across the Channel, Roland was a constant solace, and in the leisure hours of that summer the first fourteen *laisses* were translated, copied, and circulated in manuscript. Afterwards the original went with me during winter and spring through France and Belgium, and returned with me to London where, in the summer months of 1919, the translation was begun again.

M. Petit de Julleville's is the only edition I have used or even seen : of Mr. Masefield's and other translations I know only by hearsay. M. de Julleville's text, with which his translation was interleaved, is in the main that of the Oxford MS., with some emendations by Müller† and himself. In the Oxford MS. there are 3,998 lines ; to these Müller added four, as follows :—

* " La Chanson de Roland." Traduction Nouvelle Rhythmée et Assonancée. Avec une Introduction et des Notes par L. Petit de Julleville. Paris. Alphonse Lemerre, Editeur 27-31, Passage Choiseul, M DCCC LXXVIII.

† " La Chanson de Roland," berichtigt und mit einem Glossar versehen, nebst Beitragen zur Geschichte der französischen Sprache, von Th. Müller. Göttingen, 1851.

Line 1615 from the Venice   MS.
     3146   Versailles ,
     3390   Paris   ,
     3494   Venice   „

I have added a fifth, which I number 1777a, from
the Venice and Paris MSS. This line is quoted in
a note by M. de Julleville. I have also followed
Müller's arrangement of the lines 1466-1670,
which are displaced in the Oxford, but not in
other MSS. The comparative result is as follows :

Laisses.

Müller, de Julleville,⎫
     and this edition. ⎬ 113-122 ; 123, 124, 125, 126
Oxford Manuscript.   115-124 ; 126, 125, 113, 114

With these precautions, my translation may, I
hope, be used as a " Companion to the Study "
of the Oxford MS.

I do not propose to discuss the operation of
the Law of Assonance on our language, beyond
suggesting that it is an operation under local
anæsthetics, which some degree of painfulness
may accompany. For variety, there are twenty-
two different vowel-endings in the original poem,
of which half are feminine or double endings.
This number I have not attempted to match.
For consonance, I know that in the old language
the predominance of vowel over consonant sounds
makes it almost always rhyme ; and in this belief
I have indulged in sequences of rhyme to which
the professors of assonance may easily take ex-
ception. I claim only that my translation is literal :
if it cannot be read with enjoyment, there is no
more to be said.

Proper names I have spelt mostly as in the
original, anglicising such words as England and
Spain—as also Rhone (1583), Toledan (1568),
and some others ; some I have further varied to
improve my assonances. I claim also the privilege

of making one or two syllables, as the metre may require, of Charles, Neimes and Guenes; and of similarly treating past participles. The vowels of "to," "the" and some other words I have treated as elided before initial vowels: "The Arch-bishop" and "The Emperour" are invariably three syllables; "That Archbishop" and "That Emperour" are four.

The light thrown by Prosody, a science that once heard my vows of lifelong service is, I find after five years spent in reading Routine Orders and writing on Army Forms, dazzling rather than illuminant. I have therefore asked the Historian of Prosody, of French and of English Literature, and (incidentally) of Criticism, to review my work in its relation to the original, asperging both with the blessings of his unexhausted pen.

Scottish Presbyterian readers may, meanwhile, like to be reminded that the whole poem can be sung, both in French and English, to the favourite tune of their metrical Psalm:

" Now Israel*may say, and that truly."

And, as of Prosody, so of Chivalry I can, after this war, speak with no certain voice. But Mr. Chesterton has shewn, as I think he only is now qualified to shew, that my work is not a mere exercise in a dead dialect, but may be read in the light of many of the aspirations, the intentions, even the despairs of to-day.

I am indebted also to some who have let them-selves be charged with my manuscript at different stages of its progress; namely, Lord Howard de Walden, Mr. C. E. Montague, Mr. J. C. Squire, Mr. Robert Graves, and Mr. Alec Waugh.

To three others, on whose sympathy I can still rely, I have dedicated this book; and, when the time comes, I will thank them.

CHARLES SCOTT MONCRIEFF.

Note on Technique

Carles li reis, nostre emperere magne
Set anz tus pleins ad ested en Espaigne,
Tresqu'en la mer cunquist la tere altaigne ;
N'i ad castel ki devant lui remaigne,
Mur ni citet n'i est remés à fraindre,
Fors Sarraguce, k'est en une muntaigne.
Li reis Marsilie la tient, ki Deu n'enaimet,
Mahummet sert e Apollin reclaimet ;
Ne s'poet guarder que mals ne li ataignet.

IT is considerably more than forty years since
the present writer first read the *Chanson de
Roland* in the original, of which the above
lines form the first section, and, up to a few
months ago, he would have said, though in the
interval he has read it often in various forms, that
a satisfactory modernisation or translation of it
was so difficult as to be nearly impossible, and
that such an enterprise in English was the darkest
tower of all. Among the considerations which
determined this opinion we have nothing, in this
particular place, to do with those affecting the
spirit of the poem. It is with the language to some,
though the least extent, with the prosodic character mainly, that it is proposed here to deal.

The above specimen of the original itself should
make it tolerably easy for any one who can get
rid of that singular terror of the unknown which
still seems to beset Englishmen as to Old English
and even Frenchmen as to Old French, to see
what has to be done. There is a language, somewhat rough and uncut, but with the grandeur of
uncut precious stones about it, and of a remark-
able sonority. There is a measure, very exact and
possessed of more definitely metrical rhythm
than modern French poetry usually aims at. And

lastly, there is the pre-eminent characteristic of
the lines of this measure, each of which is strikingly
" single-moulded " as the word has been used
of English—that is to say, held up at the end, and
constructed all through so as to run to that end
and stop. This arrangement is neither " blank "
—that is to say disregardful of, and in fact shunn-
ing, any agreement of vowel sound at the end ;
nor rhymed—that is to say, constructed with
couplet or some other arrangement so as to effect
consonance of sound ending ; nor stanzaed—
that is to say, shaped in corresponding sets of
rhymed or even unrhymed verses. It consists of
bundles—to use the least flattering term—of lines
—bundles quite arbitrary in size or number, but
closely connected by assonance—that is to say,
identity of vowel sound in the last syllable, but
independent of the agreement in consonantal
clothing which rhyme requires.

Now, the difficulty of competition under the
first of these heads—that of language—rests upon
all competitors in modernising or translating,
and indeed is only an intense form of the general
difficulty of translation itself. I do not propose to
say much about it, though I think Captain Scott
Moncrieff has wrestled well with it. It is the
metrical and generally prosodic character which
is so specially hard to retain. Translators have,
naturally enough, tried all sorts of outflankings in
their attack ; but the worst point of these is that
the adventure is not achieved, only evaded. If
you do not convey the steady, fearless, ruthless
tramp of the single line repeating itself ; if you
fail to reproduce the dropping fire of the assonance
with its strangely combined advantage of repeti-
tion in the individual *laisse* or bundle, and free-
dom from monotony both in character and in
quantity of sound in the several *laisses*—you do
not give the effect of the *Chanson de Roland* to
those who do know it, while you give something

else to those who do not. Prose, even rhythmed prose is a flat refusal ; blank verse loses half, and the most characteristic half, of the effect ; couplet substitutes something foreign and very difficultly reconcilable ; regular stanza something more of the same kind ; while rhyme in any form alters, and in the case of the longer *laisses* has a terrible tendency, both in French and English, to " overdraw its account." The very latest French version, M. Henri Chamard's (of which a notice by the present writer appeared in the *Athenæum* for September 5th, 1919) tries different rhymes, some of them rather free according to orthodox standards, in the same *laisse*. But this not merely alters, but actually destroys, the music of the single assonance throughout.

In his directer grapple with the problem Captain Scott Moncrieff has had advantages in regard to the single line which few Frenchmen, except Agrippa d'Aubigné and Victor Hugo, have ever been able to reach. Our earlier Elizabethans gave us the single-moulded line in perfection : and the thud of the iamb (Marlowe trochaically scanned provokes a mixture of laugh and shudder) rises to the final assonance note with perfect effect. But, of course, it is in the attaining and retaining of that assonance note itself that the work, and the labour, and the crown of both lie.

I confess that, as I hinted at the beginning of this paper, I was, until very recently, under the impression that the attainment was difficult and the retainment impossible—first, owing to the peculiar obstacles to assonance in English, and secondly, because of its doubtfully agreeable effect even when obtained. If I say that Captain Scott Moncrieff has not wholly converted me, I shall only, I hope, be speaking with the frankness allowable between old professor and old student ; if I add that he has brought me a long way towards conversion I am sure I use that other frankness which befits the scholar whether old or young. It seems to me that this is not merely in detail but in general effect, the most faithful version I have ever seen of the great Song that Turoldus did something absolutely uncertain with.*

The obstacles to assonance in English, and its probable disagreeables, are many and various. In the first place (and no wise person will minimise or misunderstand this) we " have not proved it " ; it has never been an accepted and familiar form with us. In the second, we know it best as a failure of something else—a slovenly or careless substitute for rhyme. Thirdly, there are certain stumbling-blocks hard to get over or avoid in the sound-habits (I never use the word phonetic if I can possibly help it) of English as a language. We are so fond of throwing back the accent that we have comparatively few words sounding fully on the ultimate. The habit of slurring vowel-sound, though not so usual with well educated and well-bred people as phoneticians seem to think, does to too great an extent deprive us of the sharp, full ringing effect that assonance requires, and that Old French, and Spanish of all times, afford. Lastly, there is the multiplicity,—valuable in itself and not to be sacrificed to any simplifying simpleton,—of our sound-values for the same vowel. All these are dangerous lions in the path (to vary the comparison), and some of them are disagreeable beasts as well as dangerous ones. Captain Scott Moncrieff has, I think, managed the stumbling blocks, and met the beasts, with a most creditable amount of skill and courage and with a very considerable success. He has had, of course, to avail himself of some licenses, none of them, however, unjustified by good precedent.

* *Turoldus declinet*. The Colophon of the Poem is a hopeless puzzle.

He has availed himself of the accenting of finals
like *'ing* and *'eth* which was common from Chaucer
to Wyatt, and did not quite cease with Surrey as
well as though not too often of Chaucerian
" French accentuation " generally. Some slight
archaisms in language pay a double debt, and
therefore justify their own borrowing doubly.
Nor does he always require these. I take for instance a *sors* of the honestest kind and light upon
Stanza XC :—

" The Franks arise and stand upon their feet,"

in which no liberty of any kind is taken with
rhythm, vocabulary or vowel-sound, and the effect
of which is excellent.

One feature only I do not like, and that is fur-
nished by the *laisses* in which the assonance is sup-
plied by the penultimate : for instance, CXXX,
where the end words are "battle," "Charlès," "vassal's," " wrathful," " damage," " army," " hereafter," " Alde," " clasp you." English is a very
queer language—one of the few points in which
foreigners are perhaps nearer the truth about it
than some of its own children—and there are all
sorts of perhaps unexpected and perhaps inex-
plicable things that it will not bear—a fact of
which some students of its prosody seem specially
ignorant. In this matter of assonance it is like
some thoroughbreds. It is suspicious of the single
assonance, and has to be carefully familiarised,
whilst it simply bucks and lashes out at the double.
At least so it seems to me.

But it also seems to me, if I may borrow the
phrase by which, actually borrowing from Seneca,
poor Ben Jonson got himself into such complicated
trouble, that there is more—very much more—
in this version to be praised than to be pardoned.
It is quite certainly nearer to the original than any
other version that I have read, and though this of

itself would cover a multitude of sins there appear to me to be, in that region of *technique* with which it has been my privilege to deal, no multitude of sins at all and a good deal of virtue.

GEORGE SAINTSBURY.

ANN ARBOR PAPERBACKS

reissues of works of enduring merit

The University of Michigan Press | Ann Arbor